THE PENGUIN CLASSICS

FOUNDER EDITOR (1944–64): E. V. RIEU

PRESENT EDITORS:

Betty Radice and Robert Baldick

PLUTARCH was one of the last of the classical Greek historians. He was born in about A.D. 45 at Chaeronea in Boeotia, where he later had a school, and in middle age he took up a priesthood at near-by Delphi.

When Nero visited Greece in A.D. 66, Plutarch was a student at Athens. He became a philosopher, a man capable of lecturing and discussing on many learned topics, and wrote a large number of essays and dialogues on philosophical, scientific and literary subjects (the *Moralia*). He adopted the philosophical standpoint of a Platonist, and frequently attacked both Stoics and Epicureans. He wrote his historical works somewhat late in life, and his *Parallel Lives* of eminent Greeks and Romans is probably his best-known and most influential work (their translation by North was used by Shakespeare as a source for his Roman plays).

Plutarch travelled in Egypt and also went to Rome, where he had many distinguished friends. The Emperor Hadrian honoured him with a government appointment in Greece, yet he always remained strongly attached to his native Chaeronea. His death probably occurred some years after A.D. 120.

REX WARNER has been a Professor of the University of Connecticut since 1964. He was born in 1905 and was a classical scholar of Wadham College, Oxford. He taught in Egypt and England, and was Director of the British Institute, Athens, from 1945 to 1947. He has written poems, novels and critical essays, has worked on films and broadcasting, and has translated many works, of which Xenophon's *History of My Time* and *The Persian Expedition*, Thucydides' *The Peloponnesian War*, and Plutarch's *Lives* (under the title *Fall of the Roman Republic*) have been published in Penguin Classics.

PLUTARCH
MORAL ESSAYS

TRANSLATED WITH AN
INTRODUCTION BY
REX WARNER
NOTES BY
D. A. RUSSELL

PENGUIN BOOKS

Penguin Books Ltd, Harmondsworth, Middlesex, England
Penguin Books Inc., 7110 Ambassador Road, Baltimore, Maryland 21207, U.S.A.
Penguin Books Australia Ltd, Ringwood, Victoria, Australia

—

This translation first published 1971

—

This translation copyright © Rex Warner, 1971
Notes copyright © D. A. Russell, 1971

Made and printed in Great Britain
by Richard Clay (The Chaucer Press) Ltd,
Bungay, Suffolk
Set in Monotype Bembo

Contents

* *
*

Introduction

* *
*

PLUTARCH's reputation has suffered greatly and, to my mind, unjustly from the asperity and fashionable prejudice of many of his modern critics. Such adjectives as 'superficial', 'second-rate', 'uncritical' are now lavished upon him instead of those other ones, 'sublime', 'salutary', 'high-principled', which used to be applied – certainly rather indiscriminately – to every one of the 'ancients' who were regarded as 'worthies', and most of them were so regarded. No one can deny the importance of Plutarch's *Lives*. Shakespeare among many others is there to indicate it. Yet even the *Lives* are often damned with very faint praise. It is grudgingly admitted that they remain exciting and readable, these qualities themselves being often suspect to the more austere critics. But 'as a historian', we are told, Plutarch is very 'second-rate' when compared with Thucydides. The same, of course, could be said of nearly every historian. And how much of the literature which we admire and enjoy would turn out to be 'second-rate' if compared with Homer or Shakespeare!

Such comparisons are unfair. Plutarch in his *Lives* is not attempting to compete with Thucydides. His subjects are not human nature, war and peace, or 'the causes of things', but are limited to the effects of nature and training on the characters of certain famous men. If one were to compare him not with Thucydides but with Lytton Strachey, say, it is not Plutarch who would appear 'second-rate'.

This volume contains five of the seventy-eight smaller

works conventionally called *Moralia*. Most of these seem to have been written, like the *Lives*, in the latter part of Plutarch's long life (A.D. *c.* 45 to *c.* 125): like his near contemporaries Pliny and Tacitus, he found his literary energies released by the fall of the Flavians and the new era of Nerva and Trajan. In much of his writing, for all its diversity of subject, a clear educational aim can be discerned: the revival of what he thought of as a specially Greek form of culture, in which philosophy, religion, and history contributed to an ideal of humanity and civilization. In his day prominent men from the Greek-speaking provinces were beginning to achieve the highest positions in the empire. He wrote for these, as well as for Roman patrons. His influence has been spectacular. Famous in his own day, remembered in the Middle Ages, he became for the Renaissance perhaps the most significant source of ancient attitudes as well as of the facts of ancient history. The reasons why he has been less popular since the early nineteenth century are two: the growth of stricter historical standards and a deeper knowledge of the primary sources for classical Greece, and also an almost universal tendency to feel bored with conventional, well-meaning moralizing of the kind that Plutarch purveys.

Plutarch's philosophy is called 'eclectic', his natural history 'derivative', his morality 'conventional'. And these adjectives are on the whole justified. It is true that Plutarch created no philosophical system as Plato and Aristotle did; that he made no important discovery as Darwin did; that his morality is that of a kindly and cultivated man with a belief in principle and education, and to that extent can be called conventional. But then, I am inclined to ask, so what? Among those whom we admire does anyone know many whose philosophy is not 'eclectic', whose knowledge is not largely 'derivative', whose morality is not on the whole 'conventional'? These adjectives should not be taken necessarily to imply any debility of

8

intellect or shallowness or insincerity of character. Certainly in Plutarch's case his philosophy, however 'eclectic', is a very real part of him; his knowledge, however 'derivative', is both considerable and a constant delight to him, since he has all the Greek passion for hearing new things; and his morality, however 'conventional', is wholly sincere, charitable and humane.

It is true that those respectable virtues are not in themselves enough to give an author the power and insight of a Plato or a Thucydides. But anyone who is interested in human nature and in history will acknowledge that humbler writers, such as Xenophon or Plutarch, have merits of their own. And students of Greek history who are conscious of the extraordinary vitality of the Greek tradition will find Plutarch particularly valuable. He writes at a period when Greece has been for a long time under Roman domination; for an even longer time the city state – Athens, Sparta, Thebes – has ceased to exist as a political or military power. The armies of Alexander, which once carried the language and culture of Greece further eastward than even Rome was to go, are now only a memory; as Plutarch tells us, in his own day the whole of Greece could not put into the field a force comparable even with the citizens' army of one city in the days of Pericles. And Plutarch is sadly and intensely conscious both of the greatness of the past and of the present facts of the depopulation of the Greek mainland and the loss of political power. He appears to have no conception of what the future had in store, of the revival of Byzantium as Constantinople, and of the emergence of a Greek-speaking eastern empire that was to be stronger and more durable than the Latin empire in the west. To him the present existence of Roman power – expressed by the Emperor, the city of Rome, and the bureaucracy – may have seemed stable. It must also have seemed to him sadly materialistic, and even for the Roman past with its legendary virtues he does not appear to feel the same reverence as he feels for the past of Greece.

His standards are emphatically Greek. If he needs a contrast with the luxury or the tyranny of the times, he does not need to turn, as his contemporaries Juvenal and Tacitus often do, to the imaginary purity of the noble savage or to the rather dubious rectitude of Roman republicans. His terms of reference are the Muses, philosophy, 'philanthropy', and the specifically Greek meanings of such words as dignity, self-control and virtue. He may write sadly about the past but, unlike Juvenal and Tacitus, his view of the present is neither bitter nor gloomy; and this is because what to him was really valuable in the past is still very much alive. No primitive inhabitant of Scotland could conceivably have made a speech like that which Tacitus puts into the mouth of the noble rebel Calgacus; the Roman Republic was really dead; but Greeks still thought and inquired and spoke as they had done in the times of Euripides, Plato and Aristotle.

The five essays translated here have been chosen with a view to giving some idea of the variety as well as the underlying unity of Plutarch's thought and interests. I have refrained from attempting any lengthy commentary partly because they seem to me to be for the most part easily intelligible, and partly because in the few instances where this is not so, I lack the knowledge to write anything intelligible myself. Plutarch may or may not have been an expert on numerology and on the semi-mystical properties of certain geometrical forms; at any rate he knows more about these subjects than I do; and I do not think that the interesting passages in 'The Decline of Oracles' are dependent on such knowledge. The dialogue, also, on the question of whether land or sea animals are the more intelligent will not, I think, add greatly to our knowledge of biology; its value is in its light-heartedness and in the delightful stories (many of which must be true) about animals. Not every bride will readily accept all the advice which Plutarch offers to the newly married; but much of the advice is worth thinking about. Only one essay is wholly serious and personal, revealing that Plutarch's way of thought is a way of life; it is the 'Letter of Consolation' addressed to his wife. He is certainly a man of letters rather than a great creative artist, but his 'letters' are truly humane.

REX WARNER
University of Connecticut
1968

SUGGESTED READING

Readable English accounts of Plutarch and his work include:
  J. P. Mahaffy, *The Silver Age of the Greek World*, Chicago and London, 1906.
  R. H. Barrow, *Plutarch and his Times*, London, 1967.
  D. A. Russell, 'On Reading Plutarch's Moralia', in *Greece and Rome*, vol. xv, 1968.
But the best general account remains:
  R. Hirzel, *Plutarch*, Leipzig, 1912; and the fullest source of information is the article 'Plutarchos' by K. Ziegler in *Pauly's Realencyclopädie der Klassischen Altertumswissenschaft*, vol. xxi, Stuttgart, 1951.

Note: In the footnotes, references to fragments of the tragedians are to A. Nauck, *Fragmenta Tragica Graeca*, 2nd ed., Leipzig, 1889. References to Pindar are generally given from B. Snell, *Pindari carmina cum fragmentis*, 2nd ed., Leipzig, 1955.

Advice on Marriage

* *
*

INTRODUCTORY NOTE

PLUTARCH here addresses a bride and bridegroom of his own circle. This is evidently a comparatively early work, for the daughter of this marriage, Clea, grew up to be a priestess at Delphi and the recipient of Plutarch's *Isis and Osiris*, one of his most important theological and philosophical works.

Much of the material is traditional. Marriage was a stock theme of philosophers and rhetoricians. The form of the book, however, is a little unusual for Plutarch, in that it consists of more or less isolated comparisons and precepts rather than a connected argument.

From Plutarch to Pollianus[1] *and Eurydice with every good wish:*

Now that the priestess of Demeter has celebrated for you the rites of our fathers and your wedding night is over, it seems to me that these words of mine, which apply equally to you both and bear their part in the bridal song, may be both useful and appropriate.

In music one of the measures for the flute was called the 'rampant horse'. This melody, it appears, aroused desire in horses and filled them with it at the moment of mating. And of the many noble things said in philosophy, nothing deserves to be taken more seriously than what concerns marriage; it throws a philosophic charm over those who are forming a life-long partnership together and makes them kind and

1. A younger friend of Plutarch, *perhaps* the L. Flavius Pollianus Aristion known from an inscription from Tithorea of A.D. 98.

gentle to each other. Now you two have been brought up together in philosophy, and so, by way of a wedding present for you both, I have made and am sending you a summary of what you have often heard. I have put things down briefly and side by side, to make them easier to remember. I pray that the Muses may stand by Aphrodite and help her! For they know that it is no more important for a lyre or a lute to be properly tuned than it is for the proper care of marriage and family life to be set to harmony by reason, mutual adjustment, and philosophy. Indeed, the ancients gave Hermes a place at the side of Aphrodite, indicating that in the pleasures of love reason is especially valuable; and they also gave a place to Persuasion and to the Graces, so that married people should have what they want from each other through persuasion and not by quarrelling and fighting with each other.

1. Solon advised the bride to eat a quince before getting into bed with her husband, and by this, I think, he meant that from the very beginning the pleasures coming from the lips and the voice should be harmonious and delightful.

2. In Boeotia after they have veiled the bride they put a garland of asparagus on her head, this being a plant with very rough spines and yet with an extremely pleasant taste. So the bride will make gentle and sweet her partnership with her husband if he does not shrink from her and get angry with her when in the early stages she is difficult and disagreeable. The people who cannot put up with girlish tantrums at the beginning are just like those who because unripe grapes are sour leave the bunches of ripe grapes for others to eat. Many newly married women, too, who get angry with their husbands in the first days find themselves in the position of people who put up with being stung by the bees, but never reach out for the honey comb.

3. It is particularly in the early days that married people should be on their guard against quarrels and scenes. Can

they not see that even in the case of newly made furniture the joints can easily be torn apart by any accident at first, but after a time, when the joints have set, they can hardly be separated even by fire or steel?

4. It is easy enough to make a blaze out of chaff, fibre, or hare's fur; but the fire goes out quite soon unless it can catch on to something else that can hold it and nourish it. In the same way the violent physical passion that flares up between newly married people should not be considered firm and enduring unless it is based on character or reaches a real state of vitality by fastening upon what is rational.

5. By poisoning the water you can catch fish quickly and take them up easily; but it is a method which spoils the fish and makes them uneatable. In the same way women who use various kinds of love potions and spells on their husbands and subdue them by pleasure end up by being married to crazy boring delinquents. Circe got nothing out of the men whom she had bewitched and had no use for them at all when they had been turned into pigs and asses; but she was passionately in love with Odysseus, who kept his head and could deal with her intelligently.

6. Women who would rather have power over fools than listen to men of sense are like people who would rather be guides to the blind than follow those who see and know where they are going.

7. Women do not believe that Pasiphaë, who was married to a king, fell in love with a bull; yet they can observe some of their own sex who cannot bear men with firm and virtuous natures and who find it pleasanter to go with people who in their combination of licentiousness and sensuality might be dogs or goats.

8. Men who are too feeble or lazy to mount their horses properly train them to bend their knees and kneel down. It is the same with some people who have married wives who are

rich or from a good family; instead of trying to improve themselves, they bring their wives down to their level, thinking that it will be easier to have the upper hand if they are humiliated. But in using the rein one ought to take account of the size of the horse, and so one should take account of the value and worth of one's wife.

9. When the moon is a long way from the sun, she looks large and bright to us; but when she comes near she fades away and hides. With a good wife it is just the opposite; she ought to be most conspicuous when she is with her husband, and to stay at home and hide herself when he is not there.

10. Herodotus[2] was wrong when he said that when a woman takes off her clothes she takes off her modesty at the same time. On the contrary a good woman will put modesty on when she is naked, and man and wife will find in their intercourse that the greatest modesty is the sign of the greatest love.

11. When music is played in two parts, it is the bass part which carries the melody. So in a good and wise household, while every activity is carried on by husband and wife in agreement with each other, it will still be evident that it is the husband who leads and makes the final choice.

12. The Sun once won a victory over the North Wind. The wind blew hard and tried to tear a man's cloak away from him; but the man hugged it closely to him and drew it all the more tightly round himself. After the wind came the sun, and in its heat the man grew first warm and then burning hot; he ended up by throwing off not only his cloak but his shirt. Most women behave like this too. If their husbands try forcibly to make them give up their luxurious and expensive habits, they will get angry and fight back all the way; but if they are won over with the help of reason, they will quietly change their ways and live within their means.

2. *History*, 1. 8.

13. Cato[3] expelled from the Senate a man who kissed his own wife in the presence of his daughter. This was perhaps going a little too far. All the same, if it is shocking (as indeed it is) for a man and wife to be seen caressing and kissing and embracing in public, is it not much more shocking for them to be attacking and insulting each other in public? To enjoy the pleasures of sexual intercourse in secret, but to criticize and blame each other and tell home truths openly and for everyone to hear?

14. A hand mirror may be decorated with gold and precious stones, but it is no good unless it reflects a true likeness. In the same way it is no good having a rich wife unless she shapes her way of life in conformity to that of her husband and brings her character into accord with his. If a happy face reflected in a mirror looks miserable, or if a sad face looks as though it were wreathed in smiles, then the mirror is inaccurate and worthless. There is no point, and no good either, in a wife who puts on a miserable look when her husband feels like being gay and carefree, or who is full of mirth and high spirits when he is in a serious mood. In the one case she is showing unpleasantness and in the other a lack of feeling. Just as lines and surfaces in the language of mathematics have no motions of their own but only in conjunction with the bodies to which they belong, so the wife should have no feelings of her own, but should share them all with her husband, whether he is serious or gay, frowning or laughing.

15. Men who do not like to have their wives eating with them are encouraging them to stuff themselves with food when they are by themselves. So too those who are not cheerful with their wives and do not laugh and have fun with them are encouraging them to look for pleasure of their own elsewhere.

16. The legal wives of the kings of Persia sit by them at

3. Plutarch, *Life of Cato the Elder*, 17.

dinner and eat with them. But when the kings want to have a gay evening and get drunk, they send their wives out and bring in the girls who make the music and the concubines. And here at least they act rightly in not allowing their wedded wives to share in their drunkenness and debauchery. So in private life if a man who is headstrong and uncontrolled in his desire for pleasure goes astray with a prostitute or a maid, his wife ought not to be angry and embittered with him. She should reflect that it is out of respect for her that he chooses another woman with whom to join in acts of drunkenness, debauchery and immodesty.

17. Kings who are fond of the arts will lead many men to become artists; those fond of learning will produce scholars and those fond of sports athletes. So a man fond of his own appearance will make his wife spend her time in beauty parlours; a pleasure-loving husband will make his wife behave immodestly like a prostitute; and the husband who loves what is good and honourable will make his wife into a woman of sense and principle.

18. A young Spartan girl was once asked whether she had yet started making advances to her husband. She replied: 'I don't to him; he does to me.' This, I think, is how a married woman ought to behave – not to shrink away or object when her husband starts to make love, but not herself to be the one to start either. In the one case she is being over-eager like a prostitute, in the other she is being cold and lacking in affection.

19. A wife ought not to make friends of her own, but to enjoy her husband's friends together with him. And the first and best friends are the gods. Therefore it is proper for a wife to worship and to know only the gods in whom her husband believes and to shut her door to all magic ceremonies and foreign superstitions. For no god can be pleased by stealthy and surreptitious rites performed by a woman.

20. Plato[4] says that the really happy state is the one where the citizens hardly ever hear the words 'that's mine' or 'that's not mine', and this is because the citizens, so far as possible, regard everything important as belonging to all of them in common. It is even more true that in marriage those words should be entirely abolished. Except that, just as doctors tell us that a blow on the left side of the body may cause us to feel the pain on the right side, so it is an excellent thing for the wife to feel sympathy with her husband in his affairs and for the husband to feel in the same way for his wife. So, as ropes twined together gain strength from one another, the two of them will each contribute his or her share of goodwill and by their joint action the partnership will be preserved. Man and woman are joined together physically so that the woman may take and blend together elements derived from each and so give birth to a child which is common to them both, so that neither of the two can tell or distinguish what in particular is his or hers. It is very right too that married people should have the same kind of partnership in property. They should put everything they have into a common fund; neither of the two should think of one part as belonging to him and the other as not belonging; instead each should think of it all as his own, and none of it as not belonging to him. As a mixture of wine and water is called 'wine' even though the larger part of it is water, so the property and the house should be said to be the husband's, even though the wife has contributed the larger share.

21. Helen loved wealth and Paris loved pleasure. Odysseus kept his head and Penelope her virtue. Therefore in the latter case the marriage was a happy and enviable one, whereas the marriage of Helen and Paris brought a whole Iliad of suffering on Greeks and Trojans alike.

22. The Roman whose friends criticized him for having divorced a virtuous, wealthy and beautiful wife reached out

4. *Republic*, 462C.

his shoe and said: 'This is good to look at too and new, but I'm the only person who knows where it pinches me.' So a wife ought not to rely on her dowry or her birth or her beauty, but rather on the things which really bring her into contact with her husband, namely conversation, character and companionship, all of which should be agreeable and pleasing and loving and not of the stiff kind which is a continual source of irritation. Just as doctors are more alarmed by fevers that arise from obscure causes and gradually gather strength than by those which can be diagnosed on obvious and clear evidence, so it is those little, hardly noticeable disagreements between man and wife which go on day after day and continuously which do most to disrupt and to ruin a marriage.

23. King Philip fell in love with a Thessalian woman who was then accused of using magic charms on him. Olympias therefore did her best to bring her into her power. But when the woman came into the queen's presence, her beauty was obvious and her conversation graceful and intelligent. Olympias then said 'Let me hear no more of these slanders! Your magic is in yourself.' In the same way a wedded lawful wife is quite irresistible if everything – dowry, birth, magic and the girdle itself of Aphrodite – is in her own person and she wins her husband's love by character and virtue.

24. On another occasion, when a young man from the court married a beautiful woman with a bad reputation, Olympias remarked: 'That man has no brains; otherwise he would not have chosen his wife with his eyes.' Marriages ought not to be made because of what one sees with the eyes or because of what one counts on the fingers either, as with some who reckon up how much money their wife will bring them instead of estimating what she will be like to live with.

25. Socrates[5] used to tell the young men that when they looked at their faces in a mirror the ugly ones should make

5. cf. Diogenes Laertius, 2. 33.

themselves beautiful by being good, and the good-looking ones should not disgrace their beauty by being bad. So it is a good thing for the housewife when she has her mirror in her hand to say to herself, if she is ugly, 'What does it matter, so long as I am good?' and, if she is beautiful, 'What does it matter, unless I am good too?' For an ugly woman has really something to be proud of when she is loved for her character rather than for her looks.

26. The Sicilian tyrant[6] once sent some expensive clothes and jewelry to the daughters of Lysander. But Lysander would not take them and said: 'All this finery, so far from making my daughters look beautiful, will disgrace them.' And before Lysander, Sophocles[7] had said this:

> There's no adornment here, poor fool, but lack of all
> Adornment and a madness in your mind.

For, as Crates used to say, 'Finery is what makes fine.' And the best finery for a woman is fine character. This does not come from gold or jewelry or scarlet but from those qualities which clothe her in dignity, rectitude and modesty.

27. When people sacrifice to Hera in her capacity as the guardian of marriage, they take out the gall and do not consecrate it with the other parts of the offering. By this the originator of the custom intended to show that in marriage there should never be any trace of bitterness and anger. The kind of astringency which may be found in a housewife ought to be health-giving and pleasant like that of wine, not bitter like the taste of aloes or medicine.

28. Xenocrates[8] was an excellent man in every way except that he had rather rough manners and Plato's advice to him

6. Dionysius I.   7. Fr. 762.

8. Pupil of Plato, head of the Academy 347–339 B.C. His thought influenced later Platonism considerably: Plutarch is indebted to him in many ways, especially in connexion with the doctrine of *daimones*: see below, p. 47.

was that he ought to sacrifice to the Graces. And I think myself that it is especially the virtuous woman who needs the help of the graces in her relations with her husband, so that, as Metrodorus used to say, 'she may live happily with him and not be irritable because she is virtuous'. The economical woman ought not to neglect cleanliness and the wife who is devoted to her husband should also show a cheerful disposition; for economy ceases to please when it is combined with dirt, as does the most proper behaviour in a wife when combined with an austere manner.

29. Wives who are afraid to laugh and have a bit of fun with their husbands in case they should appear forward and immodest are no better than those who will not use oil on their hair in case they should be thought to be using perfume, or will not even wash their faces in case people should think they are using rouge. We notice that those poets and speakers who try to express themselves without vulgarity, meanness or affectation use all their skill to gain and hold the attention of their audience by means of their subject matter, their management of it and the moral impression which they make. And so the housewife also, just because she very rightly avoids and objects to all kinds of ostentation, forwardness and showing-off, ought to be all the more careful in her relations with her husband to show her skill in the graces of character as expressed in day-to-day life, and so establish a relationship which is honourable and pleasant at the same time. But if a woman is naturally of a forbidding, uncompromising and ungracious disposition, her husband should show understanding. When Antipater told Phocion to do something which was neither honourable nor proper, he replied 'You cannot have me as a friend if you want me to behave like a lackey.' So a husband who has a wife who is virtuous and uncompromising ought to reflect 'I cannot live with the same woman both as a wife and as a mistress.'

30. It was an ancient custom in Egypt that the women should not wear shoes and this was in order that they should stay at home all day. So with most women; if you take from them their gilded shoes, bracelets, anklets, purple dresses, and pearls they will stay at home.

31. Theano[9] once exposed her arm while she was putting on her cloak. Someone said 'What a beautiful arm!' and she replied 'But it is not for the public.' Not only the arm, but the speech of a virtuous woman ought to be 'not for the public'; in front of outsiders she should regard her words as an exposure and should be modest and careful with them; for her feelings, character and disposition are all revealed in her conversation.

32. In his statue of the Aphrodite of the Eleans Pheidias made her with one foot standing on a tortoise, thus indicating to women the virtue of staying at home and not talking. A wife should do her talking either to or through her husband, and should not take it to heart if, like the flute-player, she expresses herself most admirably through an instrument other than herself.

33. When a rich man or a king honours a philosopher, he is conferring distinction not only on the philosopher but on himself. But a philosopher who pays court to a rich man loses reputation himself without adding any to that of the rich man. It is the same with women. If they let their husbands take the first place, they themselves are honoured; but if they want to take control themselves, they make a worse impression than those who are controlled by them. And the kind of control to be exercised by a husband over his wife should be like that not of a property-owner over his property, but of the soul over the body, an affair of sympathy and of a gentle and kindly welding together. Just as it is possible to take good care of the body without being a slave to its pleasures and desires,

9. The wife of Pythagoras.

so it is possible to have authority over one's wife and at the same time make her happy and contented.

34. Philosophers distinguish three kinds of physical objects: (1) those like a fleet or an army, which are composed of separate elements, (2) those made of component parts, as a house or a ship, and (3) those with an organic unity, as have all living creatures. It is much the same with marriage. A couple who are in love with each other form an organic unity; those who marry for the sake of a dowry or in order to have children form a union of component parts; and those who merely sleep in the same bed form merely a connexion of separate individuals who would be described more correctly as sleeping together than as living together. Scientists tell us that when liquids are mixed together the mixture is total and entire. It should be the same with married people – a mutual blending of bodies, property, friends and relations. Indeed what the Roman law-giver had in mind, when he prohibited an exchange of presents between man and wife, was not to deprive them of anything, but to make them feel that everything belonged to both of them together.

35. In the African city of Leptis there is an old custom that on the day after her marriage the bride sends to her husband's mother and asks her for a pot. She does not give it and says that she hasn't got one, the idea being that the bride should recognize from the beginning a step-motherly attitude in her mother-in-law and, if something worse happens later on, should not be angry or resentful. A wife ought to realize what the position is and try to do her best about it. Her mother-in-law is jealous of her because her son loves her. And the only way of dealing with this is for her to win her husband's affection for herself and at the same time not to detract from or lessen his affection for his mother.

36. It would appear that mothers have the greater love for their sons because sons are able to help them, and fathers love

their daughters more because the daughters need their help. But it may also be because of the respect which wife and husband have for each other that each partner wants to make it clear that he or she particularly admires and loves the qualities most characteristic of the other. There may perhaps be differences here, but what is very nice to see is the wife showing rather more deference and consideration for her husband's parents than for her own and, if she has any grievance, referring it to them without mentioning it to her own parents. For if one shows trust, one is really trusted, and if one shows love, one is loved.

37. The generals ordered the Greeks in Cyrus's army to remain silent if the enemy advanced against them shouting, but to charge at them shouting themselves, if they came on in silence. Sensible women too will keep quiet when their husbands are shouting out in anger, and when their husbands are silent will comfort and soothe them with their conversation.

38. Euripides[10] rightly disapproves of lyre-playing at drinking parties. We need music when we are angry or sad and not as an added spice to the pleasure we are already having. So you must see that it is wrong for people who are in the habit of sleeping together for pleasure to go off and sleep separately, if they have had some sort of angry quarrel. It is just on these occasions that they should particularly call upon the help of Aphrodite, who is the best physician in these cases. This, no doubt, is what Homer meant when he makes Hera say:

> I will settle their strife and divergence,
> Bringing them back to their bed will join them together in love.[11]

39. At all times and in all places wives and husbands should try to avoid quarrelling with each other, but they ought to be especially careful of this when they are together in bed. There

10. *Medea*, 190 ff.   11. *Iliad*, 14. 205, 209.

was a woman in labour who, when the pains were on her, kept saying to those who were trying to get her to bed 'What's the good of going to bed? It was by going to bed that I got this.' But it is not easy to escape the disagreements, harsh words and anger that may arise in bed except just then and there.

40. I think that Hermione is speaking the truth when she says:

Bad women called upon me and they ruined me.[12]

But this does not happen quite so simply. It is only when disagreements with the husband and jealousies have induced a wife not only to let such women into the house but to let their words into her mind. It is just at these times that a sensible woman should stop her ears and be on guard against whispered gossip, so as not to add fresh fuel to the flame. She should be quick to remember what Philip said. He, we are told, when his friends were inciting him against the Greeks on the grounds that though he had treated them well they always spoke ill of him, replied 'And what would happen, if we treated them badly?' So, when these tale-bearers say 'Your husband has a good and loving wife and he treats her disgracefully,' the wife should reply 'And what would happen, supposing I was to start hating him and wronging him?'

41. A man had a slave who ran away. Some time later he caught sight of the slave and ran after him, but the slave got away from him by taking refuge in a treadmill. Upon which the master said 'That is exactly the place where I should have liked to find you.' So a wife who because of jealousy is applying for a divorce and is in a state of misery ought to say to herself, 'Isn't this exactly how my rival would like to see me, and isn't this just what she'd like me to be doing – getting angry and bitter with my husband, and giving up even my own home and my own bedroom?'

12. Euripides, *Andromache*, 930.

42. The Athenians have three ploughing festivals: one at Scirum, to commemorate the most ancient of sowings; one in Raria; and one, the 'Ox-yoking', near the base of the Acropolis. But the most sacred of all such rites is the sowing and ploughing practised in marriage for the procreation of children. Sophocles has a fine expression for Aphrodite – 'fair-fruited Cytherea'.[13] So both husband and wife should take special care about this aspect of marriage, should keep themselves pure from all wrong or criminal intercourse with other people, and should not sow seed which they would prefer sterile or which, if anything did come from it, they would be ashamed to own and would try to keep secret.

43. The orator Gorgias[14] once read a speech to the Greeks at Olympia on the subject of concord. Melanthius remarked 'This fellow is giving us advice on concord; but he has not yet managed in his private life to get just three people – himself, his wife and his maid – to live in concord.' (It appears that Gorgias was rather attracted by the maid and his wife was jealous.) So a man who is going to bring harmony into politics, business and his personal relations ought to see that there is real harmony in his own household. What most people notice is not so much mistakes made in the treatment of women as the mistakes made by the women themselves.

44. They say that cats are excited to the point of madness by the smell of perfume. Now, supposing that women too were driven out of their minds with frenzy by perfume, it would be a shocking thing for their husbands, instead of abandoning its use, to allow their wives to suffer in this way just for the sake of their own fleeting pleasure. As it is women do suffer like this, not because of their husbands using perfume but because of their having affairs with other women. Is it not

13. Fr. 763.
14. Of Leontini, the first great composer of ornamental or 'display' oratory. Little is known of his 'Olympia' speech (?408 B.C.).

wrong, therefore, to cause them so much pain and anguish just for the sake of a few moments of pleasure? Bees are supposed to get angry with and attack men after they have been sleeping with a woman; and so a husband should approach his wife just as he would a swarm of bees, that is to say pure and clean from any contact with other women.

45. People who go near elephants avoid highly coloured clothes and people who go near bulls do not wear red, since these colours have a most infuriating effect on the animals; and they say that tigers, when surrounded by the noise of drums, go completely mad and tear themselves to bits. So with men; some cannot bear the sight of scarlet and purple dresses, while others hate the noise of cymbals and drums. Is it much of a hardship then for women to do without such things and instead of irritating and upsetting their husbands to live with them quietly and graciously?

46. Philip was once trying to force a woman to come to bed with him, and she said 'Let me go. All women are the same when the light is out.' This is an excellent thing to say when dealing with lustful and violent men; but in the case of a wedded wife it is just when the light is out that she should not be the same as any ordinary woman. Instead, when her body is invisible, her virtue, her sense of belonging to her husband, her constancy and her affection should be most apparent.

47. Plato's advice to the elderly was to behave in a particularly respectable manner in the company of young people, so that the young should treat them too with respect; for if their elders show no sense of shame, there is nothing to make the young behave respectfully or modestly towards them. Husbands ought to bear this advice in mind and show more respect to their wives than to anyone else, remembering that it is in the bedroom that their wives will learn to behave either with restraint or with a total lack of it. The kind of man who enjoys pleasures which he would rather his wife did not

enjoy is no better than a man who tells her to fight to the death against enemies to whom he himself has already surrendered.

48. With regard to the love of fine clothes and furniture I should like you, Eurydice, to read and memorize the advice given by Timoxena[15] to Aristylla.

And, Pollianus, don't imagine that your wife will refrain from unnecessary display and extravagance, unless she sees that you yourself despise these things in others and are not delighted at the sight of gold drinking cups, frescoes on the walls, trappings for mules and fine neckbands for horses. It is quite impossible to drive out extravagance from the wife's part of the home when there is every evidence of it in the man's rooms.

Then, too, Pollianus, you are already at the right age to study philosophy. What you should do is to beautify your character by taking part in discussions which require careful thought and logical demonstrations, and you should try to meet and get to know the kind of people who can help you in this. Like the bees, you should gather valuables from every source, carry them with you and then share them with your wife, discussing everything with her, familiarizing her with all the best things which you have heard and getting her to love them. For to her, as Homer says,[16]

> You are a father and also her mother,
> Yes, and a brother too.

But it is a finer thing still for a man to hear his wife say 'My dear husband,

> But to me you are[17]

guide, philosopher and teacher in all that is most beautiful and most divine. In the first place these studies will take away a woman's appetite for stupid and irrational pursuits. A

15. Presumably Plutarch's wife.
16. Andromache to Hector, *Iliad*, 6. 429.
17. Adapted from Homer, loc. cit.

28

woman who is studying geometry will be ashamed to go dancing and one who is charmed by the words of Plato or Xenophon is not going to pay any attention to magic incantations. And if anyone claims to be able to draw the moon down from the sky, she will laugh at the ignorance and stupidity of women who believe in such things, since she herself has some knowledge of astronomy and has read about Aglaonike, the daughter of Hegetor of Thessaly, who knew all about total eclipses of the moon and, being able to foretell the time when it would be overtaken by the earth's shadow, imposed on the women of Thessaly by getting them to believe that it was she who was drawing the moon down from the sky.

It is said that no woman can produce a child without the co-operation of a man, yet there do exist mis-shapen growths in the womb which have the appearance of flesh. They develop from some infection and grow into a kind of consistent body. They are known as 'moles'. One should be very careful to see that nothing of this sort takes place in women's minds. For if they do not receive the seed of a good education and do not develop this education in company with their husbands they will, left to themselves, conceive a lot of ridiculous ideas and unworthy aims and emotions.

And I want you, Eurydice, to try especially to live in the company of the sayings of the wise and good, and always to have at the tip of your tongue all those things which you used to listen to with such pleasure when you were a girl and staying with us. In this way you will make your husband happy and you will be admired by other women for your adornments, which although they cost nothing will be altogether remarkable and splendid. You cannot own or wear this rich woman's pearls or that foreign woman's silks without paying a great deal for them; but you can, without paying anything, wear the finery of Theano; Cleobulina;

Gorgo, the wife of Leonidas; Timocleia, the sister of Theagenes; the Claudia of the old days; Cornelia, the daughter of Scipio; and of all the other women who have become admired and famous. And with these adornments you will live a life of honour and of happiness.

Sappho, because she wrote poetry so beautifully, had sufficient confidence in herself to write to a rich woman as follows:

> Dead you will live and no one will remember
> You ever were.
> For in the roses of Pieria
> You have no share.[18]

Should it not be even more permissible for you to think well and highly of yourself, if you have a share not in the roses but in the fruits which the Muses bring and kindly bestow upon those who love and admire education and philosophy?

18. Sappho, fr. 55, in E. Lobel and D. L. Page (eds.), *Poetarum Lesbiorum Fragmenta*, Oxford, 1955.

The Decline of the Oracles

* *
*

INTRODUCTORY NOTE

THIS is one of four substantial dialogues, the scene of which is set at Delphi, which deal with religious and philosophical problems. The narrator is Lamprias, Plutarch's humorous and lively brother; the conversation he relates is dated to a Pythian festival, probably that of 83–4; the work itself is considerably later, and presumably belongs to Plutarch's main burst of activity in the first decade or so of the second century.

The dialogue has a complex structure, which a brief analysis may help to clarify:

31

21–22 Cleombrotus resumes his discourse, and caps the stories with one of his own, about a wonderful prophet living near the Red Sea. This prophet, among other things, taught that there are 183 worlds.

(C) 23–37 Long digression on the problem of the number of worlds.

(D) 38–44 The conversation returns to divination, but is now concerned with more general theory. Lamprias makes the main contribution.

45–51 Ammonius objects to him that he is attaching too much importance to physical causes – vapours and exhalations. Lamprias, who has no wish to appear materialistic in outlook, and who is shocked at seeming to be disrespectful to the gods, modifies his views to meet this.

The dialogue is rich in fable, humour, and eloquence; some of the theorizing is both fantastic and difficult to interpret, but the main interest of the piece is fortunately not in its most obscure parts.

CHARACTERS IN THE DIALOGUE

LAMPRIAS: Plutarch's brother

DEMETRIUS: a grammarian who has travelled in Britain*

CLEOMBROTUS: a Spartan who has travelled widely in the East

AMMONIUS: the leading Athenian Platonist of his time; Plutarch's much-respected teacher

PHILIP: a writer

DIDYMUS: a Cynic philosopher

HERACLEON: a Megarian (who also appears in *The Intelligence of Animals*)

1. My dear Terentius Priscus, there is a story of how some eagles or swans flew from the ends of the world towards its centre and met at Delphi at the 'omphalos', as they call it.

* His visit seems to be attested by an inscription found at York in which a Demetrius makes a dedication to 'Ocean and Tethys', and to 'the gods of the imperial praetorium'.

And at a later date Epimenides[1] of Phaestus, to test the truth of this story, asked the god about it. The reply he got was vague and ambiguous and he said:

> So there was never a point midway in the earth and the ocean,
> Or, if there is, it is known to the gods and is unknown to mortals.

Probably the god regarded him as one who tries to test a painting by rubbing it with his fingers, and was telling him to keep his hands off the ancient myth.

2. However, in our own days, just before the Pythian games held when Callistratus was in office, it did happen that two religious and civilized men, coming from opposite ends of the known world, met together at Delphi. One was Demetrius the grammarian, who was on his way home from Britain to Tarsus, and the other was Cleombrotus of Sparta, who had travelled widely in Egypt and in the country of the Troglodytes and had sailed beyond the Persian Gulf. He was not a merchant, but a man who liked seeing the world and acquiring knowledge. He had enough money to live on and saw no point in having more than enough; and so he spent his spare time as I have said and was engaged in writing an account of what he had seen which was to be the basis for a philosophical study directed towards theology, as he himself called it. He had recently been at the shrine of Ammon and had obviously not been greatly impressed by most of the things he saw there; but he did have something very interesting to say about the lamp there which never goes out. The priests told him that this lamp uses up less and less oil every year and this they regard as a proof that the years are not all of the same length, but that each is always shorter than the one before; for it is natural that in less time less oil should be used up.

3. We were all surprised to hear this, and Demetrius said

1. Cretan prophet who visited Athens in the sixth century B.C.

that it was quite ridiculous to draw such vast conclusions from such inconsiderable evidence; it was not so much the case of reconstructing 'the lion from one claw', as Alcaeus says, as of using a wick and a lamp to reconstitute the whole spatial universe and to do away with the whole science of mathematics.

'Neither of those arguments', said Cleombrotus, 'is likely to disturb the people there. They would not agree that the mathematicians have any superiority in accuracy; on the contrary, they would say that in dealing with those remote movements and revolutions of the heavenly bodies mathematicians are more likely to make a miscalculation with regard to a period of time than are the men who measure the quantity of oil consumed and who are constantly checking it and giving it their close attention just because of the strangeness of the phenomenon. And, Demetrius,' he went on, 'to say that great things cannot be deduced from small conflicts with much of our scientific thinking. It would mean dismissing many demonstrations and predictions. Yet you grammarians, having found the word "razor" in Homer,[2] will tell us that this indicates the interesting fact that the heroes in those days used to shave; and will also tell us that they lent money on interest, because Homer says somewhere that 'a debt is owing, not recent or small', a phrase which implies the accumulation of interest.[3] And when he describes night as 'swift', you seize on the adjective with delight and say that its meaning is that Homer is describing the shadow cast by the earth as conical, being caused by a spherical body. Furthermore, if you are going to say that great events cannot be indicated by small things, you will have to reject the medical inference of an unhealthy summer from the numbers of spiders' webs that appear or from the fig leaves in spring when they grow like crows' feet. You will have to deny that

2. *Iliad*, 10. 173.   3. *Odyssey*, 3. 367.

34

the magnitude of the sun can be reckoned by reference to small measures like a quart or a gill and that in this sundial here the inclination of the acute angle, which its shadow makes with the level plane, can be described as a measurement of how far above the horizon is the ever visible pole. These are the arguments which you could have heard there from the priests. So we must find some other answer to give them, if we want to prove the certain validity of our established theories about the course of the sun.'

4. The philosopher Ammonius was one of those present and he said: 'It is not only a question of the sun, but of astronomy in general. If their argument were correct, it must follow that the sun's course from solstice to solstice must be getting shorter and shorter and will not continue to occupy so large a part of the horizon as mathematicians tell us it does; for the southern part of its track will be constantly contracting, so bringing it nearer to the northern part; our summers must become shorter and with lower temperatures, as the sun turns about within narrower limits and touches fewer parallels of latitude at the solstices; it could no longer be possible to see what is in fact observed at Syene, where the upright rods on the sundial cast no shadow at all at the time of the summer solstice; many of the fixed stars must have gone below the horizon and some must be touching each other or have coalesced, since the distance between them will have disappeared. If, on the other hand, they maintain that, while all other bodies have fixed motions, the sun alone is irregular, they will not be able to produce any reason why, among so many other bodies, only the sun is affected by this acceleration; they will cast doubt on most of our observations and make those that concern the moon completely unintelligible. So, if they want to prove the difference they need not bother about measures of oil. It will be amply demonstrated by eclipses, since it is here that the sun most frequently casts a

shadow on the moon and the moon on the earth. All this is surely clear enough, and there is no need to say any more to expose the worthlessness of their argument.'

'All the same,' said Cleombrotus, 'I saw the measurements with my own eyes. They showed me a great number of them, and the one for last year was considerably smaller than the ones from the distant past.'

'Would you say, then,' Ammonius went on, 'that this fact has simply not been noticed by all those other peoples who from time immemorial, one might say, have been tending and keeping alive ever-burning fires? Assuming that what they say is true, would it not be better to ascribe the cause to some kind of coldness or humidity in the air, which would naturally make the flame burn feebly and not need or use up much fuel? Or, on the contrary, might it not be caused by heat and lack of humidity? I have heard people say that fire burns best in winter, because then the cold forces it to contract and grow intense, whereas in hot weather it becomes feeble, thin and slack, and if it is burning in the sunlight it does even worse, not really getting hold of the fuel, and burning it up more slowly. Better still, one might say that the cause is in the oil itself. It is likely enough that in former times the oil, being made from young trees, was watery and full of incombustible material, whereas later, when the trees were fully grown and the olives mature, it was more concentrated so that an equal quantity had more strength and burned better than in the past. Why not say this, if the people at the shrine of Ammon must stick to this extraordinary theory of theirs?'

5. When Ammonius had finished speaking, I said 'What I should like to hear, Cleombrotus, are your views about the oracle. In the past the divinity in the place had a tremendous reputation, but now it looks as though all this is rather fading away.'

As Cleombrotus made no reply and kept his eyes on the

ground, Demetrius said: 'There is no need to make inquiries or raise questions about what is happening there when we can see how the oracles here are fading away, or rather how they have all, with one or two exceptions, entirely ceased to exist. Should we not rather examine this point – what is it that has caused their collapse? One need only mention Boeotia, which in the old days used to ring with the voices of oracles. But now they have disappeared entirely. It is as though the streams have dried up and a great drought of prophecy has come over the land. It is only in the neighbourhood of Lebadea nowadays that Boeotia has anything to offer to those who want to dip their pitchers into the wells of prophecy. As for the other prophetic shrines, some are silent and others are totally deserted. Yet at the time of the Persian wars there were plenty of famous oracles. That of Ptoan Apollo was as well known as that of Amphiaraus. Mys,[4] it appears, consulted both of them; and the prophet of the oracle, who in the past had always given replies in the Aeolic dialect, on this occasion spoke in a language other than Greek and delivered a reply which was unintelligible to everyone present except Mys himself. This example of the priest's prophetic frenzy made it clear that it is impossible for foreigners even to receive a reply in Greek when they are dictating to Greeks as subordinates.

'Then there was the case of the slave who was sent to the oracle of Amphiaraus. When asleep in the shrine he dreamed that a servant of the god appeared to him and first of all attempted by word of mouth to make him leave the place, telling him that the god was not there. Then he tried to push him out; and finally, when the slave still would not leave, he took up a large stone and hit him on the head with it. All this corresponded to what was going to happen. For Mardonius

4. A foreign (Carian) emissary of Xerxes. See Herodotus, *History*, 8. 133–5.

was defeated by the Greeks under the leadership of one[5] who was not a king, but a guardian and deputy of a king; and he fell, struck by a stone, just as the Lydian slave dreamed that he himself had been struck.

'It was also at this time that the oracle of Tegyrae was at the height of its fame. It is actually said that this place was the birthplace of Apollo; there are two streams that flow past it and up to this day the people there call one of them "the Palm" and the other "the Olive". In any case, at the time of the Persian wars, when Echecrates was priest there, the god prophesied victory for the Greeks. And in the Peloponnesian war, when the people of Delos had been driven out of their island, it is said that they received an oracle from Delphi telling them to find the place where Apollo was born and make certain sacrifices there. They were surprised and quite bewildered at the idea that Apollo could have been born anywhere other than in Delos, but then the Delphic priestess gave them another oracle, telling them that a crow would show them the way. So they went away and got as far as Chaeronea. Here they heard the woman who kept their inn talking about the oracle to some strangers who were on their way to Tegyrae. As they left these strangers said good-bye to the woman, addressing her by her name which was "Crow". The Delians then understood what the oracle had meant, made their sacrifices at Tegyrae, and soon afterwards found that they could return to Delos. There have been other and more recent manifestations of divinity at these shrines, but now the oracles have vanished. It seems worthwhile, therefore, now we are in the precinct of Pythian Apollo to inquire why it is that this change has taken place.'

6. By this time we had gone past the temple and had

5. Pausanias, regent of Sparta and guardian of the Spartan King Pleistarchus.

The reference is to the battle of Plataea in 479 B.C.

reached the doors of the Cnidian Clubhouse.[6] So we went inside and found the friends whom we were going to see sitting there waiting for us. It was generally a quiet time as at this hour people were either having a clean-up after their exercise or watching the athletes.

Demetrius smiled all round and said: 'Am I to tell the truth, or tell a lie?'[7] It doesn't look to me as though you have anything very important under discussion. I see you all sitting there with relaxed faces and perfectly at ease.'

'True enough,' Heracleon of Megara replied, 'we are not trying to find out which of the two "l's" in the verb "ballo"[8] is the one that it loses in the future tense, nor from what positives are derived "worse" and "better" and "worst" and "best". Subjects of that sort do no doubt make people look grim; but one can examine other subjects in a philosophic spirit without necessarily drawing one's eyebrows together in a frown and can discuss them dispassionately without glaring at other people and getting angry with them.'

'Then let us join you,' said Demetrius, 'and bring with us a subject for discussion which has come up quite naturally in connexion with the place where we are and which, since it concerns the god, concerns all of us. And there is no need to frown and look grim while you are dealing with it.'

7. So we joined their party and sat down with them. Demetrius put forward the subject for discussion and immediately Didymus the Cynic, who is nicknamed Planetiades,[9] sprang to his feet, gave the ground two or three blows with his stick and burst out: 'Wonderful! So this is the

6. This *lesche* was a rectangular building divided into three aisles; the walls were decorated with famous murals by Polygnotus (fifth century B.C.) which survived to Plutarch's time (cf. Pausanias 10. 25, 31).

7. Homer, *Odyssey*, 4. 140.

8. Present βάλλω (I throw). Future βαλῶ.

9. 'Wanderson', a nickname suggesting vagabond habits.

subject you have brought to us which is so difficult to understand and requires so much thought! There has been such a
flood of wickedness all over the earth that, as Hesiod[10] said
long ago, Shame and Righteous Indignation have fled from
the life of men; and now you find it surprising that also
Divine Providence has packed up the oracles and disappeared
from every place where they once were. On the contrary,
what I should like to discuss is why the oracle here still
functions, and why another Heracles, or some other god,
has not snatched away the tripod. For it is now taken up
entirely with shameful and irreverent questions put to the god
by people who are either testing the validity of his pre-
tensions or asking about property or legacies or illegal
marriages. This is incontrovertible proof of how wrong
Pythagoras was when he said that men are at their best when
they approach the gods. What in fact happens is that men bring
quite openly and unashamedly into the presence of the god
those maladies of the soul and emotional disturbances which
it would be proper to disown and conceal in front of an older
man.'

He was ready enough to go on talking, but Heracleon gave
a tug at his coat and I, who perhaps got on better with him
than any of the others, said 'My dear Planetiades, you mustn't
make the god angry; for he is a mild and gentle god and, as
Pindar says, "He has been judged to be the kindest of gods to
mortals."[11] And whether he is the Sun itself or the lord and
creator of the sun and of all that extends beyond our vision, it
is not likely that he should think that men of the present time,
for whose birth and growth and very existence and ability to
think he is himself responsible, are unworthy to hear his
voice. Nor is it likely that Providence, who like a good and
kind mother watches over us and does everything for us,
should be mean and niggardly only in the matter of prophecy,

10. *Works and Days*, 199–200.　　11. Fr. 149.

when it was she who gave it to us in the first place. You would not suggest that in the old days, when oracles were established all over the world, there were not even more wicked men to be found, since there were more men altogether in the world. So come and sit down again. Make a Pythian truce[12] with wickedness (which you are always inclined to castigate with your tongue) and help us to look for some other reason which will account for what we call the eclipse of oracles. But don't provoke the god. He is kindly and well disposed to us.'

My words did at least have some effect; for Planetiades went out through the doors without saying another word.

8. There was silence for a few moments, and then Ammonius turned to me. 'Consider what we are doing, Lamprias,' he said, 'and give the subject your full attention. We must not deny responsibility to the god. For if anyone thinks that the disappearance of those oracles which now no longer function was caused not by the will of a god but by something else, we will come to suspect that in his view those oracles were not established and maintained by the god, but were otherwise caused. Prophecy is in fact the work of a god, and there is no greater or more powerful force than god to do away with and abolish it.

'I do not approve of what Planetiades said and I particularly disapprove of his attributing inconsistency to the god. For according to him the god will turn his face from wickedness in one direction and reject it, and in another direction will welcome it, as though he were some king or dictator who bars some of his doors to evil-doers, but lets them in freely at others and transacts business with them. Now the qualities which we must necessarily attribute to all actions of the gods are these: moderation, adequacy, excess in no direction and perfect self-sufficiency in all. And I think that the logical way

12. The general armistice kept throughout Greece during the days of the Pythian Games at Delphi.

of dealing with our question would be to start from this point
and admit that in the general decline of population which has
taken place throughout nearly all the inhabited world as the
result of the wars, civil and international, which have been
fought in earlier times, Greece has suffered more than any
other country. Today the whole of Greece could scarcely
raise a force of three thousand hoplites, which was the number
sent by one city, Megara, to fight at Plataea. Thus the fact
that the god's presence has been withdrawn from many
oracular shrines is merely a proof of the desolation of Greece.
What good would it be if there were an oracle at Tegyrae, as
there used to be? Or at Ptoeum, where for most of the day you
will hardly see a single shepherd with his flocks? As for this
oracle here at Delphi, which is the oldest and the most famous
of all, they say that for a long time the place was deserted and
unapproachable because of a fierce monster, a snake,[13] which
lived there. But to attribute the inactivity of the oracle to the
presence of the snake is to take things the wrong way round.
It was not the snake that caused the desolation of the place; it
was the desolation that attracted the snake.

'When by God's will Greece grew strong, with many cities
and a population spreading all over the land, they used to
employ two priestesses, who took it in turns to go down into
the shrine; and there was a third one appointed to act as a
reserve. But now there is only one priestess, and we do not
complain, since one is enough to meet the need. So there is no
reason at all to blame the god. The prophetic art as it exists
today is sufficient for everyone and capable of giving satis-
factory answers to all who consult it. Even with nine heralds
Agamemnon had difficulty in keeping the assembly of his
troops in order, because there were so many of them; but
here in a few days' time you will see that in the theatre one

13. An obscure story: elsewhere (*The Face in the Moon*, 945B)
Plutarch speaks of Typhon overthrowing the oracle at Delphi.

announcer can make his voice carry to everyone. So in the old days prophecy employed more voices to reach more people. But today it is just the opposite. Indeed we should be surprised at the god if he allowed prophecy to run to waste, like water, or to echo in the wilderness as the rocks echo with the cries of shepherds and the bleating of their flocks.'

9. I remained silent when Ammonius had finished speaking, and Cleombrotus turned to me and said, 'So, Lamprias, you have already admitted this point – that it is the god who both creates oracles and does away with them.'

'No,' I said, 'I have not. I maintain that no prophetic shrine or oracle is done away with by the action of the god. It is the same here as with many things which he creates and provides for us. What puts an end to some of these things is Nature, or rather the very matter from which they are composed which is itself a disintegrating force and is constantly reverting to its first state and slipping away from the form imposed upon it by an agency stronger than itself. It is the same, I think, with the forces of prophecy. There will be periods when they grow dim and when they fade away entirely. For the god gives many good things to men, but nothing that is immortal. As Sophocles says, "The works of gods may die, but not the gods." [14] Wise men are always telling us that we must look for their presence and their power in nature and in matter, and that it is to the god that we must, as is right, ascribe the first cause. And it is utterly absurd and childish to imagine that the god behaves like those ventriloquists (they used to be nicknamed "Eurycles", [15] but are now called "Pythons") and enters into the bodies of the prophets, speaking through them and using their mouths and voices as his instruments. For if he becomes involved in the wants and

14. Fr. 766.
15. Eurycles was a famous ventriloquist mentioned by Aristophanes and by Plato.

necessities of men, he is throwing away his own majesty without regard for the value and worth and magnitude of his perfection.'

10. 'You are right,' said Cleombrotus, 'but it is hard to understand and to determine precisely just how and to what extent Providence should be brought in. And so it is equally erroneous and an exaggeration to say that absolutely everything or that nothing at all is caused by divine intervention. True that there is much good sense in the view that Plato, in discussing the element which underlies all created qualities (what we now call "matter" or "Nature"), freed philosophers from a number of serious difficulties. But I think that still more and still greater difficulties have been cleared away by those who have assumed that there is a race of daimons half way between gods and men and who have found a force to fasten together in a way and to confirm our community with the divine. This is a doctrine that may come from the Zoroastrian magi, or it may be Thracian and go back to Orpheus, or it may be Egyptian or Phrygian, as looks likely when we observe the religious rites in both lands, where so much that is connected with mortality and mourning has a part in their sacred celebrations. But of the Greeks it seems that Homer used the word differently; there are times when he speaks of the gods as "daimons". It was Hesiod[16] who first clearly and distinctly defined four classes of rational beings – first gods, then daimons, then heroes, and finally men. And it is from this classification, it would appear, that he derives his idea of the change from the race of gold to a race of many good daimons, and from a race of demi-gods to a race of heroes.

'Others maintain that souls as well as bodies are subject to

16. The texts of Hesiod and Plato (*Symposium*, 202–3) were commonly used to support the belief in these semi-divine intermediate beings.

transmutation. Just as we see that water is generated from earth, air from water, and fire from air, as their substance is carried upwards, so the better souls are able to ascend from men into heroes and from heroes into daimons. And from among the daimons a few souls, purified by the long exercise of virtue, have been able to share fully in the divine nature. But to some of these souls it happens that through lack of self-control they slip backwards and are clothed again in mortal bodies and have a dim shadowy life like exhalations from the ground.

11. 'Hesiod thinks that even the daimons end their existence after a certain passage of time. Speaking in the person of the Naiad, he gives us an indication of how long this time is:

> Nine generations of men in their vigour will equal the cawing
> Crow's life-span. And the stag lives four lives of the crow.
> Three life-spans of stags will bring old age to the raven.
> Nine of the raven's spans the Phoenix lives and we, fair-tressed
> Daughters of Zeus, the Nymphs, live ten spans of the Phoenix.[17]

Now those who misinterpret the word "generation" will add this up to a tremendous sum. In fact the word means "year" and so the life-time of the daimons is 9720 years – less than what most mathematicians think, but more than what Pindar says when he speaks of the Nymphs as

> Allotted a life-time as long as a tree's.[18]

And this is why he calls them "hamadryads".'

At this point Demetrius interrupted and said, 'How can you say, Cleombrotus, that what is meant by a "generation" is a "year"? One cannot give this as the length of the life of a man either "in his vigour" or "in his age", as some read the passage. Those who read "in their vigour" make a generation equal

17. Fr. 304, in R. Merkelbach and M. L. West (eds.), *Fragmenta Hesiodea*, Oxford, 1967.

18. Fr. 155.

thirty years, in accordance with Heraclitus, this being the time in which a father can have a son who is also a father. But those who prefer "in their age" to "in their vigour" say that there are 108 years to each generation; in their view the middle years of man's life are reached at the age of fifty-four, a number made out of the first number, the first two plane surfaces, two squares and two cubes,[19] which are the numbers Plato used in his 'Generation of the Soul'.[20] In fact the whole of this passage from Hesiod seems to be referring to the conflagration,[21] when all liquids will disappear and with them no doubt the Nymphs,

> Who in the beautiful forests
> Dwell and the fountains of streams and the thick green grass of the
> meadows.'[22]

12. 'Oh yes,' said Cleombrotus, 'this is what I hear from a lot of people and I notice that the Stoic conflagration, just as it feeds on the verses of Heraclitus and Orpheus, is now taking hold of Hesiod's too. But I can't stand this talk about the total destruction of the universe, and the weight of such impossibilities must be borne by those guilty of the exaggeration evident in such statements, particularly in those about the crow and the stag. Does not a year include within itself the beginning and the end of "all that the Seasons and the Earth produce"? And is it not contrary to men's usage to call this a generation? You yourselves, I imagine, agree that Hesiod uses the word "generation" to mean a man's life-time. Do you not?'

'Certainly,' said Demetrius.

19. $1 + (1 \times 2) + (1 \times 3) + 4 + 8 + 9 + 27 = 54$.
20. *Timaeus* 35A–C.
21. The Stoics believed in a periodic destruction of the universe by fire.
22. Homer, *Iliad*, 20. 8–9.

'This also', said Cleombrotus, 'is clear – that the measure and the things measured are often called by the same names. For instance gill, quart, gallon and bushel. We call unity a number, it being the smallest number and the first. And we use the year as the first measure of man's life. So, in just the same way, Hesiod, employing the same word for the thing measured, has called the year a generation. Moreover the numbers arrived at by those who interpret the word differently have none of the great and splendid qualities which we expect to find in numbers. But the number 9720 has been arrived at by adding together the first four numbers and multiplying them by four,[23] and when this is multiplied five times by three, it gives the number already mentioned.[24] However, there is no need for us to quarrel with Demetrius on these points. For whether the period of time in which the soul of the daimon or hero suffers a transmutation of life is longer or shorter, determinate or indeterminate, there will still be evidence, supported by the wisdom of the past, to prove his point that there exist as it were on the frontiers between gods and men certain natures, which feel human emotions and are subject to the laws of change. And it is proper for us, as our fathers did before us, to consider these as daimons, to address them by that name and to honour them.

13. 'Xenocrates, the friend of Plato, made use of the shapes of triangles to illustrate this point. He compared the equilateral triangle to the nature of the gods, the scalene to that of men and the isosceles to that of the daimons. For the first has all its sides equal, in the second they are all unequal and in the third they are partly equal and partly unequal like the nature of the daimons, which has human emotions and godlike power. And nature has set before our eyes perceptible images and likenesses – the sun and the stars for the gods, and rays of light,

23. $(1 + 2 + 3 + 4) \times 4 = 40$.
24. $40 \times 3^5 = 9720$.

comets, and meteors for mortal men. Euripides makes use of this comparison when he writes:

> Who yesterday was strong of flesh falls from the sky,
> Quenched like a star that breathes its spirit to the air.[25]

But in the moon we find a complete body which has a real resemblance to the daimons; it is in accord with the cycles through which those beings pass; it is subject to wanings, waxings and transformations which are evident to the eye; and, seeing this, some call the moon an earth-like star, some a star-like earth and others call it the domain of Hecate who has power both on the earth and in the heavens. Now suppose one were to do away entirely with the air between the earth and the moon, the result would be the dissolution of the unity and conjunction of the universe, since there would be nothing in the middle except empty and unconnected space. In just the same way those who will not accept the existence of the race of daimons leave no kind of bond or interconnexion between gods and men and abolish what Plato calls the "interpretative and ministering nature".[26] Either this, or else they force us into total confusion and complete disorder by dragging the god down to the emotions and activities of man, making him descend to the level of man's needs, just as the women of Thessaly are supposed to be able to draw the moon down from the sky. In fact Aglaonice, the daughter of Hegetor, did get the women to take this disgraceful piece of deceit for truth. She was a good astronomer, they say, and whenever there was an eclipse of the moon, she used to pretend that she was drawing it down from the sky by her enchantments. But as for us, let us not listen to anyone who says that there are some oracles not divinely inspired or religious initiations and rites in which the gods take no part; but on the other

25. Fr. 971.
26. cf. *Statesman*, 260 D and *Symposium*, 202 E.

hand we must not imagine that the god is actually there at these ceremonies in the sense of walking about at them and conducting them. Instead we should rightly attribute all this to those ministers of the gods who act as servants and recorders of the divine. We should believe that it is the daimons who watch over the rites of the gods and celebrate the mysteries, while others of them go about the world punishing acts of pride and great injustice. And there are others whom Hesiod very impressively addresses as

Holy
Givers of wealth and having in this a right that is royal,[27]

by which he implies that it is kingly to do good. For among daimons, just as among men, there are different degrees of goodness. In some of them a residue or survival of the emotional and the irrational is still to be found, though weak and dim; while in others this residue is considerable and hard to destroy. And embedded in various sacrifices, mystic rites and legends throughout the world traces and symbolic references to these facts are preserved and guarded.

14. 'The clearest expression and intimation of the truth about daimons is to be gained from the Mysteries, but on them, as Herodotus[28] says, "my lips must be sealed in reverence". But there are some festivals and sacrifices, very like days of gloom and ill-omen, in which we find the eating of raw flesh, the tearing apart of the victims, fasting, beating of breasts and also, in many places, the use of obscene language at the shrines and

Madness and yells of the roused in excitement,
Head-tossing furious din.[29]

These things, I should say, are not done in honour of any god, but are designed to placate and appease in order to avert evil

27. *Works and Days*, 122, 126.
28. *History*, 2. 171.
29. Pindar, *Dithyrambi*, ii, 12–13.

daimons. It is incredible that the gods ever demanded or welcomed the human sacrifices of the past; nor could kings and generals have surrendered their own children, consecrated them to sacrifice, and cut their throats on any other supposition than that they thought they were propitiating and offering satisfaction to the heavy, cruel anger of merciless and savage avenging spirits, or to the mad tyrannical lusts of beings without either the power or the wish to make contact with humanity in or through the body. Heracles laid siege to Oechalia for the sake of a girl; and so there are powerful and violent daimons who demand a human soul incarnate in a body and, until they get what they desire, they bring plagues and famine to cities and stir up war and civil strife. Sometimes, however, the opposite happens. Once, for instance, when I was spending a considerable time in Crete, I observed them celebrating a strange kind of festival in which they were exhibiting the figure of a headless man. This, they say, was once Molus, the father of Meriones, who had raped a young girl and was then discovered to be without a head.

15. 'As for the stories and hymns which men tell or sing, about how one or other of the gods carried off property or went wandering or into concealment or exile or bondage, these were not the afflictions nor the fortunes of gods but of daimons, and it is because of their great virtues and powers that they are remembered. Aeschylus speaks irreverently when he says:

> Holy Apollo, god exiled from heaven.[30]

So does Admetus in Sophocles' play:

> My cock it was that sent him working at the mill.[31]

But it is the theologians of Delphi who stray furthest from the truth in believing that once upon a time there was a battle

30. *Supplices*, 214.   31. Fr. 767.

here between the god and a serpent for the possession of the oracle. And they allow poets and prose-writers to tell this story in their competitions in the theatre, though in doing so they are directly contradicting the most sacred of the religious rites performed here.'

This statement came as a surprise to Philip the historian, who was one of the company, and he asked what holy rites were contradicted by the competitors.

'The ones that have to do with the oracle here,' said Cleombrotus, 'and in which Delphi has recently initiated all the Greeks west of Thermopylae and has carried them as far as Tempe. For the hut that is put up here near the threshing-floor every eight years, far from being a representation of the nest or lair of a serpent, is in fact a copy of the dwelling of some great lord or king. Then there is the attack made upon it in silence; the Labyadae,[32] with lighted torches, lead the boy, who must have two parents living, along the path known as "Dolon's Way"; they set fire to the hut, overturn the table and flee through the doors of the temple without looking back; then finally there are the wanderings of the boy, his servitude and the rites of purification which take place at Tempe. All this seems to suggest that some terrible act of violence was done in the past and brought pollution. For it is quite absurd, my dear friend, to suppose that Apollo, after killing a reptile, should run away to the ends of Greece in need of purification, and should then, when he got there, offer libations, and do all those things that men do to cleanse themselves and placate those spirits called the "unforgetting avengers", because they chase after the memories of the stain of unforgettable and ancient crimes. As for the story which I have heard so far about this flight and departure from one

32. An uncertain (conjectural) reading. For the festival, see Plutarch, *Greek Questions*, 12; J. E. Harrison, *Prolegomena to Greek Religion*, 2nd ed., p. 113 f., Cambridge, 1907.

place to another, it is curiously nonsensical and inconsistent. But if it does contain any vestige of truth, we must not imagine that what took place in those days in connexion with the oracle was anything unimportant or in the common run of things. But I don't want you to think that I am behaving in the way that Empedocles describes,

> Putting together the heads of different
> Stories, and never reaching one road's end.[33]

So let me add the fitting conclusion to what we said at the beginning. In fact we have already reached it. I think that we too should venture to say, as many others have said, that with the total disappearance of those daimonic powers responsible for oracles and places of prophecy, the oracles too will disappear and will lose their power, since these powers have fled away or gone somewhere else; but when after many years these powers return again, then the oracles, like musical instruments, will find their voice, since those who can use them are present and taking care of them.'

16. When Cleombrotus had finished, Heracleon said, 'There are no irreligious and blasphemous people here, and we all hold views about the gods which are very much alike. Nevertheless, Philip, I think that we ourselves ought to be careful that we do not, without realizing it, accept some very strange and far-reaching assumptions in dealing with this subject.'

'You are quite right,' said Philip. 'But which of Cleombrotus' suppositions is the one that upsets you?'

'I think', said Heracleon, 'that it is not unreasonable to suppose that it is not the gods but the daimons, acting as ministers of the gods, who have charge of oracles, since it is right that the gods should be freed of earthly concerns. But

33. Empedocles, Fr. B. 24, in H. Diels and W. Kranz (eds.), *Die Fragmente der Vorsokratiker*, 6th ed., Berlin, 1954.

to take, practically by the handful, from the verses of Empedocles instances of sin and blind delusion and wanderings imposed by heaven, and to say that all these things happened to the daimons, and to end up by supposing that they die, just as men do – that really does seem to be going too far in rather an uncivilized direction.'

Cleombrotus asked Philip who this young man was and where he came from. Then, when he had heard his name and the name of his city, he said, 'We do realize, Heracleon, that our argument is leading us along strange paths; but in dealing with important matters it is impossible to get near the probable truth in our conjectures without making use of far-reaching principles. You yourself, however, have failed to realize that you have conceded a point and then taken it back again. You agree that daimons exist; but in claiming that they are neither wicked nor mortal you no longer allow them to be daimons. For in what way can they differ from the gods, if in regard to being they are not subject to dissolution and in regard to virtue they are not subject to emotion or to sin?'

17. While Heracleon was thinking this over in silence, Philip said, 'We hear of wicked daimons, Heracleon, not only in Empedocles, but in Plato, Xenocrates and Chrysippus. Democritus too, when he prays to meet with "propitious spirits", clearly recognizes that there are spirits of a different kind which are unpropitious, impelled to evil and choosing evil instead of good.

'As to whether beings of this sort can die, I heard a story from an intelligent and reliable source. Some of you have listened to the orator Aemilianus.[34] Well, his father was Epitherses. He was a native of my city and was my teacher in literature. He told me that he had once made a voyage to

34. Identification uncertain. For the story of the death of Pan see especially Rabelais, *Pantagruel* IV. 28 (Pan = Christ).

53

Italy on a merchant ship which carried a number of passengers. Near the Echinades Islands late in the evening the wind dropped and the ship drifted near Paxi. Nearly everyone was awake, and a number of them were still drinking their wine after dinner. Suddenly from the island of Paxi they were astonished to hear the voice of someone calling out loudly for Thamus. Thamus was an Egyptian pilot, and not many even of those on board knew his name. He was called for twice and made no reply, but the third time he answered. The caller then raised his voice and said, "When you come opposite Palodes, tell them that Great Pan is dead." Epitherses told me that when they heard this everyone was amazed and they discussed whether it would be better to do as they had been asked or let things be and do nothing about it. In the end Thamus decided that if there was a breeze, he would sail past and say nothing; but if the sea was smooth near the place and there was no wind, he would make the announcement that he had heard. So when he came opposite Palodes and there was no wind or wave he looked out from the stern towards the land and spoke the words as he had heard them: "Great Pan is dead." And before he had finished speaking a great wailing arose, not from one voice but from many, and mingled with the wailing were cries of amazement. As there were many people on the ship, the story was soon told in Rome and Thamus was sent for by Tiberius Caesar, who was so convinced of the truth of the story that he had a careful inquiry made about Pan. The opinion given by the numerous scholars at his court was that Pan was the son of Hermes and Penelope.'

As it happened there were several of those present who could bear Philip witness, having attended the lectures of old Aemilianus themselves.

18. Demetrius then told us that among the islands off the coast of Britain there were a number scattered in the sea and

practically uninhabited which were called by the names of various daimons and heroes. He himself, on the emperor's instructions, had made a voyage of exploration to the nearest of these desolate islands, which was inhabited only by a few holy men, all of whom were treated with reverence by the Britons. Soon after his arrival there was a tremendous storm and many strange sights were to be seen. Great gusts of wind tore the air and lightning flashes darted down to earth. When it was all over, the people of the island said that some great soul had passed away. 'Just as there is nothing terrible', they said, 'about a lamp when it is being lit, but many people are disturbed when it is put out, so it is with great souls. Their kindlings into life are gentle and harmless, but their extinctions and dissolutions very often, as we have just seen, bring on great winds and storms and often infect the air with plague and disease.' They also said that in those parts there was one island where Cronus is imprisoned;[35] he is watched over by Briareus while he sleeps, for the bonds set on him are those of sleep, and there are a number of daimons around him to act as servants and attendants.

19. Cleombrotus now spoke. 'I too', he said, 'could tell you stories of the same kind as this. However, for the purpose of our argument it is sufficient that there is nothing to contradict or to prevent things from being as we have stated. Yet we know that the Stoics not only hold the view that I have mentioned with regard to the daimons, but also maintain that among the gods, of whom there are a very great number, there is only one who is eternal and immortal; all the rest they believe to have come into existence and to be liable to extinction.

'As for the Epicureans, we have no reason to be frightened of their mockery and jesting which they actually turn against Providence itself, saying that it is only a myth. We declare

35. A similar story in Plutarch, *The Face in the Moon*, 941 A.

on the contrary that their "infinity" is a myth implying, as it does, that among all the countless worlds there is not one that is directed by divine reason, but that they all owe their creation and continued existence to pure chance. If there is any place for laughter in philosophy, then what is really laughable are those "images" of theirs, dumb, blind and soulless, which they herd together for countless cycles of years, and which keep on putting in their appearance everywhere, some floating away from bodies which are still living and others from bodies which have long ago been burned or fallen into decay. This is to drag shadows and old wives' tales into the study of nature. And yet these philosophers get very upset if anyone maintains that daimons exist, not merely for physical reasons, but for logical reasons, and that they have the power to exist and go on existing for long periods of time.'

20. Ammonius spoke next. 'It seems to me', he said, 'that what Theophrastus said is quite right. And what indeed is there to prevent us from accepting a pronouncement which is so impressive in itself and so truly philosophical? Reject it and you will have to regard as impossibilities many things which are possible, but cannot be proved; accept it and you will at the same time be doing away with many impossibilities and unrealities. The one argument that I have heard put up by the Epicureans against the view of daimons as stated by Empedocles is that if they are happy and long-lived, it is impossible that they should be evil and vicious, since evil is full of blindness and apt to give way to destructive forces. This is a stupid argument and would imply, for instance, that Epicurus was a worse man than Gorgias the sophist, and Metrodorus a worse man than Alexis, the comic poet; for Alexis lived twice as long as Metrodorus, and Gorgias more than a third as long again as Epicurus. When we say that goodness is something strong and evil something weak, we are using the words in a different sense altogether and not

referring to physical longevity or dissolution. We observe, for instance, even in the animal world that there are many slow-moving and slow-witted creatures and many creatures that are untameable and savage which live longer than creatures that show intelligence and versatility. It is therefore wrong to maintain that God's eternal existence is the result of careful precaution and the repelling of destructive forces. On the contrary, to be immune from emotion and destruction must be inherent in the very nature of the Blessed Being, requiring no kind of effort or activity. However, it is perhaps inconsiderate to be addressing our words to people who are not here to answer them. So let us ask Cleombrotus to take up again from the point where he left it a moment ago the argument about how the daimons leave one place and reappear in another.'

21. 'And I shall be surprised', said Cleombrotus, 'if what I say now does not seem to you much stranger than what has been said so far. Nevertheless it seems relevant to the science of nature and we shall find a hint of it in Plato,[36] who without making any unqualified statement on the subject does give some hint of the opinion towards which he is groping. He does this with caution, but that has not prevented a great outcry against him by other philosophers. But we have, as it were, a mixing bowl set before us for our common use in which are blended all kinds of myths and stories, and where could one find such kind people to listen to these stories and to test them just as one tests foreign currency? So I shall not be afraid to give you the benefit of a story I heard from a man, not a Greek, whom I had great difficulty in finding and only found after long travel and after paying out a lot of money. It was near the Persian Gulf. Here once every year this man meets with human beings, the rest of his time being spent, according to his own account, in the company of wandering

36. cf. section 22.

nymphs and daimons. Here I had the opportunity of speaking
to him and was most kindly received by him. He was the best-
looking man I have ever seen, and he never had a moment's
illness. Once every month he used to take some of the fruit of
a kind of plant. It is bitter and has medicinal qualities. He
spoke a number of languages, but with me he usually con-
versed in a Doric dialect which was almost like music. While
he was speaking, the whole place became fragrant, the breath
from his mouth being like a very sweet perfume. He had
always at his disposal a great fund of learning and a wide
knowledge of history, but one day each year he was inspired
with the gift of prophecy and then he would go down to the
sea and foretell future events. Rulers and the emissaries of
kings would come on these occasions and would then return
to their countries. Now it was to the daimons that this man
attributed his prophetic power. In particular he had much to
say about Delphi and indeed he was acquainted with all the
stories told and with all the ceremonies performed here.
These stories and rites too, he said, referred to the tremendous
experiences of daimons, as also did those with regard to the
Python. It was not true that the slayer of the Python was
exiled for eight years and afterwards sent to Tempe. In fact
after his expulsion he went into another world, from which
after eight cycles of the Great Years he returned purified and
indeed Phoebus, "the Shining One"; and so he took over the
oracle which all this time had been under the care of Themis.
We find the same thing in the stories about Typhons and the
Titans; these were battles of daimons against daimons,
followed by exile for the vanquished or punishment inflicted
by a god upon the sinners – upon the sin, for example, which
Typhon is said to have committed against Osiris, or Cronus
against Uranus. Honours used to be paid to these daimons, but
these honours became dim to us or faded away entirely, when
the daimons themselves were removed to another world. I

find, indeed, that the Solymi[37] on the Lycian frontier used to pay particular honour to Cronus; but after he had killed their rulers, Arsalus, Dryus and Trocobius, he fled away and went somewhere else (they cannot say where), and after that they paid no further attention to him; but Arsalus and the others are called "the stern gods" and the Lycians, both as individuals and as a state, use their names in calling down curses. Theology[38] will provide us with many other stories of the same kind. "But," as the man I was speaking of said, "if we call some daimons by the names usually given to gods, there is nothing to be surprised about in that. For each of them is naturally named after that god with whom he is allied and from whom he had received his due portion of power and honour." We find in fact among ourselves that one man is named Dius, another Athenaeus, another Apollonius or Dionysius or Hermaeus; but only some of these, and by chance alone, have been named correctly; most have been given names derived from the names of gods which are simply a play on words and have no bearing on the people themselves.'

22. Cleombrotus now was silent and we all thought that he had told us some most remarkable things. Heracleon then inquired in what way this was related to Plato and the hint he had provided about these beliefs. 'You are sure to remember', Cleombrotus replied, 'that Plato emphatically rejected the theory of an infinite number of worlds, but he was in some doubt about whether or not there was a limited number of them. Up to five he would allow to be a reasonable supposition – one world to correspond with each of the elements – but he himself kept to one. This view seems to be peculiar to

37. Mentioned by Homer, cf. *Iliad*, 6. 144; but much of this story is obscure.

38. A variant reading gives 'mythology'. In any case Plutarch means 'tales about the gods'.

Plato.[39] All the other philosophers have been terrified of the idea of plurality. They have felt that if, instead of limiting matter to one world, they went beyond one, they would immediately be faced with the problem of the unlimited and the difficult notion of infinity.'

'But what', I said, 'did this foreign friend of yours have to say on the subject? Did he put a limit to the number of worlds, as Plato did? Or when you were with him, did you not try to find out his views on the point?'

'You can be sure', said Cleombrotus, 'that on those subjects I would have been specially anxious and keen to listen to him, when he was so kind as to give up his time and attention to me. What he said was that there are not an infinite number of worlds, nor is there one world, nor five; the number is 183 and the worlds are arranged in the form of a triangle, with sixty worlds on each of the three sides; the three remaining worlds are set one at each angle and those that are next to each other are in contact and move round each other in a kind of gentle dance. The space inside the triangle is the common hearth of all and is called the Plain of Truth. In it lie undisturbed the reasons, the forms and the patterns of all that has been and all that will be; and all round them is Eternity, from which Time, like a stream, flows into the worlds. Once in ten thousand years human souls, if their lives have been good, may see and contemplate these things; and the best of the initiatory rites in this world are nothing but a dream of that revelation and that initiation; and all our philosophic reasoning here is a mere waste unless it is done to recall to our minds the beauties that are there.

'This was the story which that man told me, and he told it just as if it were a form of initiation into the mysteries, without offering any demonstration or proof of what he said.'

23. I now turned to Demetrius and asked him, 'How does

39. See *Timaeus*, 55C–D.

that passage about the suitors go, when they are looking in wonder at Odysseus while he is handling the bow?' Then, when he had reminded me of it, I said, 'I think I might say the same thing of your foreign friend:

Surely he had an eye for things and was given to stealing.[40]

And what he stole were opinions and stories from all over the place. He was much travelled in literature and was not a foreigner at all, but a Greek and with a very good knowledge of Greek culture. What shows him up is the figure he gives for the number of worlds. This is not a figure that comes from Egypt or India; it is Dorian and comes from Sicily; it was the idea of a man from Himera called Petron.[41] Personally I have never read Petron's own treatise and do not know whether it is still extant; but Hippys of Rhegium, who is mentioned by Phanias of Eresus, tells us that this was what Petron believed and what he said – that there are 183 worlds in contact with one another according to element; he fails, however, to explain what is meant by "in contact according to element", and gives us no further enlightenment on this point.'

Demetrius now joined in. 'But how could he have given us more enlightenment on these subjects? Even Plato merely set down his own statement without trying to prove it or make it probable.'

'All the same,' said Heracleon, 'we find that you grammarians attribute this view to Homer, when you say that he divided the universe into five worlds – heaven, water, air, earth and Olympus.[42] Of these five he leaves two to be held in common – the earth for all below and Olympus for all above

40. Homer, *Odyssey*, 2. 397.

41. A Pythagorean. Phanias (or Phainias) of Eresus, presumably the source of all this, is a Peripatetic who flourished *c*. 300 B.C. Hippys of Rhegium may be a fiction.

42. Homer, *Iliad*, 5. 187.

– and the three intermediate worlds were assigned to the three gods. In the same way it would appear that Plato[43] took the most perfect and original forms and figures of things, and associating them with the different divisions of the universe called them five worlds – one of earth, one of water, one of air, one of fire and lastly the world of the dodecahedron, which includes all of these in its great expanse and versatility; and it is especially to this world that he gives a form consonant and harmonious with the cycles and movement of the soul.'

'Why should we bring Homer into this?' said Demetrius. 'Haven't we had enough of myths? And Plato in fact is very far from saying that the five divisions of the world are five different worlds. In those passages where he is arguing against those who assume that there are an infinite number of worlds, he states that in his opinion this one world of ours is the only-begotten and beloved of the god, and that it was created whole, entire and sufficient to itself out of the totality of corporeal nature. It would be very surprising, therefore, if after having set down the truth himself he should supply others with a starting point for theories that are both un-convincing and irrational. For to abandon the idea of a single world did somehow or other imply the assumption of the infinity of the universe; but to put a definite limit to the number and say that there are neither more nor less than five is a wholly irrational procedure with no sort of probability about it. That is,' he added with a glance at me, 'unless you have something to say.'

'It looks to me', I said, 'as though we have now given up our discussion about the oracles, as if we had finished with that subject, and have embarked upon another topic which is just as difficult.'

'No,' said Demetrius, 'we have not given that one up. We are merely not passing over this other subject which has come

43. cf. Plato, *Timaeus*, 31A and 55C.

up. We will not spend long on it, and only touch on it just so far as to see whether there is anything to be said for it. Then we will go back to the original proposition.'

24. 'Well, then,' I said, 'in the first place those considerations which prevent us from assuming an infinite number of worlds need not deter us from assuming that there are more than one. It is possible for God and prophecy and Providence to exist in more worlds than one and for the element of chance to be minimized and for most things and the most important things to come into existence and suffer change in accordance with a fixed order – all of which is precluded by the notion of infinity. It is also more reasonable to suppose that this world is not the only-begotten of God and quite by itself. For God, being totally and entirely good, cannot be lacking in any virtue and certainly not in those which have to do with justice and kindness, which are the noblest of all and appropriate to gods. There must then be other gods and other worlds in relation to which he exercises those virtues which imply a community. For no use at all can be made of justice or kindness or goodness merely in relation to himself or to any part of himself; they demand the existence of others. So it is not likely that this world is tossed to and fro in an infinite void, friendless and isolated and unrelated. Do we not observe in nature that individual things are all included in classes and species, as seeds are in pods and seed-vessels? In the whole list of existing things there is nothing that does not fall into some general category, nor is anything put into a category unless it has certain qualities either in common with others or else in itself. Now the world is not spoken of as having qualities in common with others. Its qualities therefore are in itself and it being what it is, came from the difference between it and other things which are like it and of similar appearance. If in the whole of nature there is no such thing as one man, one horse, one star, one god, one daimon, why should we say

that there is just one world and not more than one? For to say that in nature there is only one land and one sea is to overlook an obvious point, namely the doctrine of similar parts; for we divide earth into parts which have similar names and so we do with the sea. But a part of the world is no longer a world; it is something combined from different elements in nature.

25. 'Some people are very prone to a kind of terror which induces them to use up the whole of matter on one world, so as not to leave anything outside which might, by resistance or collision, disturb the composite structure. But this fear is unjustified. If there are more worlds than one, and if each of these has been given its proper portion of matter and substance in the right qualities and within the right limits, then there will be nothing left over which is unorganized or uncontrolled, no kind of wastage which might come crashing in from outside. The reason governing each world is in control of the matter of which each world is constituted and so will not allow anything to be swept away from it and go wandering off to crash into another world, nor anything out of another world to crash into it, since in nature quantity is not infinite or unlimited and motion is not irrational and unorganized. Even if emanations do pass from world to world, there will be nothing discordant about them; they will be kindly influences, able to unite peaceably with all parts of nature, like the beams of starlight which blend together; and the worlds themselves must take delight in gazing at each other with friendly eyes, while all the good gods which are in each of them will enjoy visiting and kindly welcoming each other. There is nothing impossible in all this or fanciful or contrary to reason – not unless one is going to take what Aristotle said[44] as indicating that there are physical reasons against it. For if, as he says, each one of the elements has its own proper place, the earth must from every direction tend towards the centre

44. cf. Aristotle, *De caelo*, 1. 7.

and above it must be the water, settled, because of its greater weight, below the lighter elements. So, if there are more worlds than one, what will happen is that in many places the earth will be shown above the fire and the air and in many places it will be below them; and the same will be true of the air and the water; in some places they will be in their proper and natural positions and in other places they will not be. And since this, in his view, is impossible, it follows that there are not two or more worlds, but only this one world which comprises the whole of matter and is established in accordance with natural law, proper to the diversity of its elements.

26. 'But though this argument looks impressive, is it true? Look at it, my dear Demetrius, in this way. His view of the motion of the different elements is this – that some move downwards towards the centre, others move upwards and away from the centre, and others move in a circular path around the centre. But what is his reference for determining the centre? He cannot mean the centre of space, since according to him there is no such thing as empty space. And if we take the view that empty space does exist, it still cannot have a centre, just as there is no point at which it may be said to begin or to end; for these are limits, and the infinite has no limits. And suppose one were to be so carried away by the argument as to venture to suggest that the infinite is in a state of motion, all the same, no difference would be made to the motion of the elements by looking at them in reference to this spatial motion. For in the infinite empty space the elements have no power of their own, no predilection or impulse to make them cling to the centre or to make them from all directions tend towards this point. What we are dealing with are, on the one side, inanimate bodies and, on the other, an incorporeal and undifferentiated position or field; and it is just as difficult to conceive of a centripetal motion originating in the bodies themselves as to conceive of a force of attraction

originating in the field. We are left therefore with the conclusion that the centre must be defined not by reference to any
place, but by reference to the bodies themselves. For this
world of ours has an organic unity which is made up of
numerous and different elements, and it is from these differences that there necessarily arises a variety of motion among
a variety of things. Evidence of this is to be found in the fact
that all change in substance is accompanied by a change in
spatial position. Dispersal, for instance, redistributes the matter
rising from the centre by whirling it round and upwards;
while condensation forces it down towards the centre and
compresses it.

27. 'On this point there is no need to say more now. The
fact is that whatever cause one may suppose to be operative
in the occurrences and changes which we have mentioned,
that cause will keep each one of the worlds together as a unity;
for each world has earth and sea; each has its own centre, its
own laws governing the movements and changes among the
elements, its own natural constitution, and a force which
preserves each one and keeps it in its place. As for what lies
beyond, whether it be nothing at all or an infinite empty
space, it can have no centre, as we have already said. And if
there are more worlds than one, each of these has its own
centre and consequently its own laws of motion, with some of
its elements moving towards the centre, some away from it
and some around it, absolutely in accordance with Aristotelian doctrine. And to maintain that where there are many
centres it is only towards one centre that all the heavy matter
will be impelled from every direction is like saying that with
many men in the world all the blood from all of them must
flow in one single vein and all the brains of all of them must
be enveloped in one single membrane – the assumption being
that there must be something terribly wrong if in the
organization of nature all solid bodies are not concentrated

in one single place and all liquids in another. That would be a ridiculous assumption and it is equally ridiculous to be annoyed at the fact that everything which constitutes a whole has its own parts which are invariably organized and placed in accordance with the order of nature. To dispute this fact would be just as absurd as to call that a world which has its moon somewhere inside it or to call something which has its brains in its heels or its heart in its head a man. But it is not absurd to say that there are more worlds than one, each separate from the other, and to classify and distinguish the parts which go with each whole. In each there will be land and sea and sky placed, as they should be, in their natural positions; and each of the worlds will have its top and its bottom and its circumference and its centre, not with reference to any other world or anything outside, but in itself and with reference to itself.

28. 'As for the stone which some people assume to exist in space outside the world, it is difficult to conceive how it can be either unmoved or in motion. If it has weight, how can it be motionless? And if it is neither a part of the world nor in the same order of being, how can it move, like other things which have weight, towards the world? But as for earth which is within the boundaries and system of another world, we recognize the natural laws involved and the tension by which each part is held together, and so there should be no reason for us to wonder why it does not, because of its weight, break away from its own world and come into our system. For if we take the words "bottom" and "top" as referring not to our world but to a point outside it, we shall find ourselves in the same difficulties as Epicurus,[45] who imagined all his atoms as moving in the direction of "under our feet", as though empty space has feet or infinity permits us to conceive of downward or upward inside itself. For the same reason we may well be

45. Fr. 299, in H. Usener (ed.), *Epicurea*, Stuttgart, 1887.

surprised at Chrysippus too, or rather we may be quite at a loss to understand what could possibly have led him to assert that the world has been firmly set in the centre and that its substance, occupying this central position from eternity, is thereby given a particular guarantee of permanence and actually made secure against the possibility of dissolution. He does in fact say this in the fourth book of his work *On Possibilities*, first having the strange illusion that there is a central point in the infinite, and then still more absurdly ascribing the cause of the permanence of the world to this non-existent centre; and this in spite of his often having stated in other works that substance is organized and held together by the motions towards and away from its own centre.

29. 'Nor should we be afraid of the other objections raised by the Stoics. They ask us how, if there are more worlds than one, there can still be only one Fate and one Providence and why there should not be many gods, all with the attributes of Zeus. Now, in the first place, if it is absurd to suppose that there are a number of supreme gods, then what the Stoics themselves believe is certainly a great deal more absurd; for in their infinite cycles of worlds they produce an infinite number of suns and moons and Apollos and Artemises and Poseidons. And in the second place, if there are more worlds than one, that does not necessarily mean that there are a number of supreme beings. Why should there not be as leader and guide and controller of each world a divine power with sense and reason exactly as is the power who among us is called the Lord and Father of all? Or why should he not be watching over and directing all of them in their turn and giving all of them their first principles, their elements of growth and the rules for all that takes place within them? There are many examples in this world of ours of a single body composed of separate bodies – an assembly, for instance, or an army or a troupe of dancers – and each member of such composite bodies has, as

Chrysippus believes, the contingent faculty of living, thinking and learning. Why, then, should it be thought impossible that in the whole universe there should be ten or fifty or even a hundred worlds, all subject to one reason and organized under one government? In fact for gods such an arrangement as this is just what we should expect. We ought not to think of gods as if they were queen bees confined to their hives, or to regard them as being enclosed or rather imprisoned in matter, as do those who consider the gods to be conditions of the atmosphere or forces of water or fire blended together and who think that they came into existence at the same time as the world and will in the end be burned up with it. According to this view the gods instead of being free and unconfined, like charioteers or pilots of ships, are like statues riveted and welded to their pedestals, enclosed and clamped down to the corporeal, and they must go along with it to the point of destruction and total dissolution and transformation.

30. 'But to my mind a grander and loftier view of the gods is to say that they are their own masters and not subject to outside control; they are like the twin sons of Tyndareus,[46] who come to the help of sailors in the storm,

> Soothing the rush of the raging sea,
> And the sudden squalls of the wind.[46]

They are sailing in the ships themselves; they appear above them and save them; and in the same way one or another of the gods will come to visit one or other of the various worlds, led there by pleasure in the sight of it and he will co-operate with Nature in keeping it on its right course. Homer's Zeus did not turn his eyes very far from the plain of Troy when he looked towards Thrace and the wandering tribes of the Danube;[47] but the real Zeus has before his eyes a beautiful,

46. Pindar, fr. 140c (the attribution to Pindar is uncertain).
47. Homer, *Iliad*, 13. 3.

a fitting and a changing scene; his attention is not concentrated on one infinite empty space, nor is it, as some people have concluded, fixed solely upon himself; instead he looks down upon the many works of gods and men and the movements and courses of the stars in their cycles. For the divine nature, so far from being averse to change, takes great pleasure in it, if we may judge from all the shiftings of place and cycles among the heavenly bodies visible to us in the sky. But infinity is entirely without sense and reason, is quite incompatible with the idea of god, and in every relation must make use of the concepts of chance and accident. On the other hand the care and the providence that is exercised within a limited group and a limited number of worlds seems to me at least in no way less wonderful or less arduous than that which has, as it were, clothed itself in one body and become attached to one body which it reshapes and remodels an infinite number of times.'

31. I had talked for some time and now I stopped speaking. Soon Philip took up the conversation. 'I should not like to assert confidently', he said, 'that the truth about this subject is exactly what you say or that it is not. However, if we do not confine the divine agency to one world, why should we say that he is the creator of five worlds and no more? And how is this number five related to the whole series of numbers? I think that I would rather have a clear understanding of this than of the meaning of the letter E set up here as a dedication.[48] For the number five does not represent either a triangle or a square; it is not a perfect number or a cube; and it does not seem to have anything else particularly subtle about it to offer to those who are fascinated and delighted by such things. The Master[49] himself did make an obscure reference to its

48. The meaning of this E was much disputed. Plutarch wrote a separate dialogue about it, in which seven different solutions were propounded.   49. Pythagoras? Plato?

being derived from the number of the elements, but this is not at all an easy point to grasp nor does it give any kind of indication as to what were the convincing reasons which led him to assert the probability that when five bodies with equal angles and equal sides and equal areas are formed from matter, five complete worlds should immediately arise from them.'

32. 'Yes,' I said, 'and Theodorus of Soli has some good remarks to make on this point in his discussion of Plato's mathematical theories. What he says is this: Plato's primary figures – the pyramid, the octahedron, the icosahedron and the dodecahedron – are all beautiful because of the symmetries and equalities in their relations, and Nature has been left with no possibility of putting together or constructing forms superior to these or even like these.[50] But they are not all formed in the same way, nor do they have a similar origin. The pyramid is the simplest and the smallest, while the dodecahedron is the largest and most complex. And of the other two the icosahedron has more than twice as many triangles as the octahedron. It is therefore impossible that they should all have originated at once from the same matter. The small, the simple and the structurally less complicated must be the first to respond to the moving and formative forces and must be brought to substance and completion before those others which are larger and compounded of many parts, like the dodecahedron, which requires more work to be put into the making of it. It follows therefore that the only primal body is the pyramid; none of the others qualify, since they are left behind by the pyramid in the process of coming into being. There must therefore be a remedy for this odd situation, and it is to be found in the division and separation of matter into five worlds – one in which the pyramid will attain substantial existence first, another for the octahedron, and another for the icosahedron; then from the one that first acquires

50. cf. Plato, *Timaeus*, 53C–56C.

substance in each world, the rest will proceed, all things being capable of mutation into all things according to the principle of the combination of parts as outlined by Plato himself, who goes into considerable detail on the subject. But we shall be content with a rough knowledge of the theory. Air is formed when fire is extinguished and again, when rarefied, gives off fire from itself; now let us observe what happens to the generative elements of each and how the transmutations take place. The generative elements of fire are the pyramid, composed of twenty-four primary triangles, and of air the octahedron, composed of forty-eight primary triangles. One primary element of air, therefore, is produced from the combination of two corpuscles of fire; and again, when divided, it separates into two corpuscles of fire, and again when compressed and condensed, it takes the form of water. So in every case the one that first acquires substance always provides the others with an easy way of coming into existence by means of transmutation. And it is not the case that only one of them is the first to exist; according to the environment any of the others may take the lead in motion and outrun the rest in coming into existence, and so the word "first" can be applied to all of them.'

33. 'Well', said Ammonius, 'I must say that in his treatment of these things Theodorus has put up a very gallant performance. All the same I shall be surprised if it does not appear that he has made use of assumptions that are self-contradictory. He claims that all five must not take form simultaneously; instead the first to come into existence must always be the simplest, the one that takes least labour to construct. And then, as though this were a natural consequence and not contradictory to what he has said already, he lays it down that not all matter brings forth first the simplest and least complicated forms; instead it is sometimes the ponderous and complex forms that take the lead and are the

first to arise from matter. And then another point: five bodies are postulated as primary, and on the strength of this there are said to be five worlds. But he only produces evidence with reference to four of these. As for the cube, he has simply taken it off the board, as though he were playing a game of draughts. For the nature of the cube is such that, since its triangles are not homologous triangles, it cannot transmute itself into the other bodies nor give them the power to transmute themselves into it. In the others the common triangle, underlying them all, is the half triangle; but in the cube, and in the cube alone, is the isosceles triangle, with no convergence towards the other and no conjunction which could bring about a unity. If, therefore, there are five bodies and five worlds, and in each only one body takes the lead in coming into existence, then where the cube has been the first to come into existence, there can be none of the others at all, since it is by nature incapable of transmuting itself into any of them. I pass over the fact that they make the primary element of what is called the dodecahedron something different and not the scalene from which Plato constructs the pyramid and the octahedron, and the icosahedron. And so', Ammonius added laughing, 'either you will have to clear up these difficulties or else come forward with some theory of your own to enlighten us all.'

34. 'At the moment', I said, 'I have nothing to say that is any more convincing than what I've just said. But it is, perhaps, better to be examined on one's own views than on those of other people. So let me go back to what I said at the beginning: that if we assume there to be two natures – one that is evident to the senses, mutable in coming into being and in dissolution, unstable, now here, now there, and another one which is essentially apprehended by the reason and always remains the same – then it is very odd of us when this intellectual nature has been subdivided and allowed to have variety in itself, to feel angry and indignant if someone

divides and separates the corporeal and passive nature, instead of leaving it as a close-knit and self-convergent unity. Surely things that are permanent and divine ought to be most closely self-connected and to avoid, so far as that is at all possible, all subdivision and separation. Yet the power of differentiation has fastened even on these things, and in the intelligible world has defined differences in reason and in idea which are greater and more important than separations in space and locations. And so Plato,[51] arguing against those who affirm the unity of the whole, says that these five things exist: Being, Identity, Differentiation, and finally Movement and Rest. Supposing, then, that these five exist, there would be nothing surprising if each of the five corporeal elements had been created as a copy and image of each of these other five – not perfect and unalloyed, but in so far as each material element has the greatest share or participation in the corresponding intelligible force. The cube is obviously a body related to Rest, because of the security and stability of its plane surfaces. The pyramid's fiery and restless quality is evident to everyone in the simplicity of its sides and the acuteness of its angles. The nature of the dodecahedron, comprehending, as it does, the other figures, may well be regarded as an image or likeness referring to all corporeal being. And as for the remaining two, the icosahedron shares mostly in the nature of Differentiation and the octahedron in that of Identity. And so the octahedron contributed air, which in a single form enfolds all being, and the icosahedron contributed water, which by blending and admixture takes on the greatest variety of qualities. If, therefore, Nature demands equality of distribution in all things, then it is reasonable to suppose that this rule holds also with regard to worlds and that neither more nor less of these have been created than the patterns, so that each pattern in each world may be the governing and dominant

51. Plato, *Sophist*, 256 C.

one, just as has happened in the construction of the primary bodies.

35. 'Let this, anyway, be a comfort to those who are astonished when we divide Nature, in its generation and change, into so many classes. But now I would like you all to give your attention to this other point. Consider the first of the numbers (I mean the number one and the indeterminate duality); the second of these is the element of all formlessness and disorder, and has been called infinity; but the nature of the number one provides a limit and a confinement to what is empty and irrational and undefined in infinity, gives it form and makes it in some way capable and receptive of definition – the next step after the recognition of perceptions. And these first principles with regard to number are apparent from the very beginning; or rather it may be said that quantity is not number at all without the concept of the number one, which like a form of matter arising from the unlimited in infinity sets apart "more" on one side and "less" on the other. And then, delimited by the number one, each of the quantities becomes number. But take away the number one and once again the indeterminate duality will throw all into confusion in a condition without rhythm, without limit, and without measure. Since form is not the doing away of matter, but the shaping and bringing to order of the underlying matter, it follows that in number also these two first principles must be present, and it is from these that the first and greatest difference and dissimilarity has arisen. The indeterminate first principle is the creator of the even, and the better one of the two is the creator of the odd. Two is the first of the even numbers and three the first of the odd numbers. From the two together comes the number five, which in composition is common to both categories but which is in its own right an odd number. For in the division of the perceptible and the corporeal into a number of parts (which followed from the

innate necessity of differentiation) the number involved could not be the first even number, nor could it be the first odd number; it had to be the third number, formed from these two, so that it might be produced in this way from both the primary principles (that which created the even and that which created the odd); it was impossible for one of these to be separated from the other, since each has the nature and the power of a first principle. So, when the two were joined together, the better of the two was dominant and checked the tendency of the indeterminate towards the dispersal of matter; by setting unity in the middle, when matter was being distributed to the two, it did not allow the whole to be divided into two parts. There have indeed come into existence a number of worlds because of the differentiation of the indeterminate and its dispersal; yet the form of Identity and of Limitation has brought it about that that number should be odd and not only odd, but that kind of odd which did not allow Nature to transgress the limit of what is best. For if the number one had been unalloyed and pure, there could have been no separation of matter at all; since, however, it has been combined with the dividing power of duality, it has been severed and divided, but at that point the process stopped, the odd being dominant over the even.

36. 'This was why in the old days counting was usually called "numbering by fives". I think too that *panta* (all) is derived from *pente* (five), and reasonably, because the pentad is formed from the combination of the first numbers. Also, when differing numbers are multiplied together, the result will be a number different from themselves. But in the case of the pentad, take it an even number of times, and it will make ten exactly; take it an odd number of times and it will reproduce itself.[52] I pass over the fact that it is the first com-

52. When multiplied by an even number, the result will end in nought; when by an odd number, in five. This number is arrived

posite of the first two squares, unity and the tetrad; and that it is the first whose square is equal to the squares of the two numbers immediately preceding it, making with them the most beautiful of the right-angled triangles; and it is the first to give the ratio $1\frac{1}{2}$:1. It may be that all this has not much to do with what we are discussing now. What is, however, more to the point is the natural separative power of this number, and the fact that Nature does distribute most things by fives. To us ourselves she has given five senses and five parts of the soul – growth, perception, appetite, fortitude and reason; also five fingers on each hand, and seed which is most productive when divided five times; for there is no record of more than five children ever being born to a woman at one birth. The Egyptians too have a story that Rhea gave birth to five gods, a story which seems to hint at the genesis of the five worlds from one single matter. And in the universe we find that the surface of the earth is divided among five zones and the heavens by five circles, two arctic, two tropic, and the equator in the middle. Five also are the orbits of the planets, if the Sun and Venus and Mercury follow the same course. The organization of the world too is based on harmony, just as of course we see that what is harmonious to us depends on the five notes of the tetrachord: lowest, middle, conjunct, disjunct, and highest; and the musical intervals are five: quarter-tone, semitone, tone, tone and a half, and double tone. It appears, then, that Nature takes more pleasure in making all things in fives than in making them spherical as Aristotle said.[53]

---

at by adding the three Platonic 'parts' of the soul (*Republic* 410 B, 440 E ff.) to the Aristotelian 'growing' and 'perceptive' elements: the result is a wholly artificial scheme, but one characteristic of the way in which later philosophers liked to combine Platonic and Aristotelian doctrines.

53. cf. Aristotle, *De caelo*, 2. 4 (286 b 10).

37. 'One may inquire why it was that Plato[54] referred the number of his five worlds to the five geometrical figures and said that God made use of the fifth construction in his final adornment of the whole universe. Then, in his discussion of whether there are more worlds than one,[55] where he raises the question whether it is correct to say that in reality one or five exist in nature, it is clear that in his view this is where the idea came from. Now to show what in all probability follows from his conception, let us remark that changes in movement must necessarily follow immediately from changes in the bodies and their shapes. This is what Plato himself teaches[56] when he shows that in all separation and conjunction the change of substance is accompanied by a change in spatial relationships. For example when fire is generated from air by the breaking up of the octahedron and its resolution into pyramids, or when air is generated from fire by being forced together and compressed into an octahedron, it is impossible for it to occupy the same space as it did before; instead it breaks out of it and is carried to some other place, fighting against and forcing its way through every obstacle that stands in its way. He describes what happens even more clearly by comparing it to "grain and chaff being tossed about and winnowed by winnowing fans and other tools used in purifying the grain", saying that in just the same way the elements toss matter about and are tossed about by it. Like always goes to like and things are now in one place, now in another, until out of the elements the whole universe has been set in order. So at the time when matter was in the state which we may reasonably suppose in a universe from which God is absent, the first five properties, each with its own particular tendency, were immediately carried in different directions; but they were not completely and absolutely separated from each other, because in a general mixture and

54. Plato, *Timaeus*, 55 C.   55. ibid., 31 A.   56. ibid., 57 C.

confusion of all things the inferior always follows the superior in accordance with natural law.[57] The result was that these five principles produced in the different kinds of bodies, as they were carried now here, now there, an equal number of separate divisions with intervals between them: one fiery, but not of pure fire; one ethereal, but not of air unmixed with anything else; another earthy, but not of earth only; and especially (as is natural considering the very close association of air with water) they arranged matters, as has been said, so that these, in their separations, should be filled with many different elements. It was not God who divided substance and settled it in different areas of space; no, it was only after it had fallen apart by its own action, and was being carried in different directions in great disorder that God intervened and set it in order by means of proportion and limitation. He then established in each one Reason as governor and guardian, and created the same number of worlds as there were primal bodies. Allow me, then, in honour of Plato, to make this offering on behalf of Ammonius. Speaking personally, however, I should not venture to assert positively that there is exactly this number of worlds. When I observe that matter is by nature divisible and has a tendency to disperse, and that it can neither remain as a unit nor is allowed by Reason to spread out to infinity, it seems to me just as reasonable to suppose that there are more worlds than one – yet only a limited and not an infinite number – as it is to assume either that there is only one world, or that there are five. We have already referred to the teachings of the Academy, and I think we should certainly remember them here and avoid leaping to conclusions. When talking about infinity we are on treacherous ground and we should just try and keep our footing.'

38. 'Lamprias's advice is good,' said Demetrius, when I had finished. 'It is true that whenever we risk making assertions

57. Or 'in spite of natural law (or nature)'.

about these things as if we really understood them "by many changing forms the Gods deceive us", and these are forms not of "trickery", as Euripides has it,[58] but in the facts themselves. "But," as the same author says, "the argument must be carried back" to the assumption with which we started. We said then that when the daimons go away and abandon their oracles, these are left idle and useless like the instruments of musicians. Now this raises another and more important question as to the causality and the force employed by the daimons to inspire the priests and priestesses with the spirit of prophecy and enable them to declare what they have seen. We cannot attribute the silence of the oracles to the disappearance of the daimons unless we feel sure we know how it is that the daimons, when they are present and in control, make the oracles active and articulate.'

Ammonius now intervened and said, 'But don't you agree that the daimons are simply souls going from place to place and, as Hesiod says, "garmented in mist"?[59] To me it seems that the difference between a soul and a soul which has put on a body appropriate to this present life is like the difference between a man acting in tragedy and a man acting in comedy. And so there is nothing unreasonable, indeed nothing at all surprising, in soul meeting soul and conveying an impression of the future. Much the same thing happens with us. We do not say everything we have to say by means of the spoken word; we also employ writing or simply by a touch or a glance of the eye we convey information about the past or intimations about the future. But it may be that you, Lamprias, can tell us something more about this. It was not long ago that we heard a rumour that you had had a long talk with some strangers in Lebadea about all this; but our informant could not give us any details.'

58. Fr. 972. The allusion that follows is in fr. 970.
59. *Works and Days*, 125.

'That was natural enough,' I said. 'It was on a day when sacrifices were being made and the oracle was being consulted and there were all kinds of interruptions and distractions, so that our talk was of a loose and desultory kind.'

'Now, however,' said Ammonius, 'you have people to listen to you who have plenty of time on their hands and are eager to seek and to gain information. No one is in an argumentative mood, no one anxious to press his own views. A sympathetic hearing and freedom of speech is, as you can see, guaranteed.'

39. As the others too joined in his request, after a short pause I began to speak again. 'As a matter of fact, Ammonius,' I said, 'it was you who happened to provide the starting point and the introduction to the conversation which you have just mentioned. According to you and to the divine Hesiod, souls which have been separated from the body or which have no connexion at all with the body are daimons, "pure spirits on earth and guardians of mortal men", as Hesiod[60] says. But why then deprive souls that do inhabit bodies of the power which the daimons have and which enables them to know and reveal the future? It is unlikely that souls, after they have left the body, gain any power or accretion not present in them before. No, they always have them; but they have them in a low degree when they are united with the body; indeed some of these powers are latent and not evident at all, while others are weak and dim, slow and heavy in movement like the faculties of people groping about in the fog or wading through water; they need careful nursing in order to recover their proper state and they need to be cleansed and purified from the coverings that overlay them. The sun does not become bright when it comes through the clouds; it is always bright, yet in a fog it looks to us dim and indistinct. So with the soul; it does not acquire the power of prophecy

60. *Works and Days*, 123.

when it comes out from the body as from a cloud; it has the power all the time, but it is blinded by being mingled and combined with what is mortal. And there is no reason for us to doubt this or to be surprised by it when we see in the soul (and indeed this is the most obvious thing of all) that faculty which is the complement of prophecy and which we call memory, and what wonderful work the memory does in preserving and retaining the past – though it would be better to say "the present" – since of all that has passed away nothing exists, nothing remains; in the very moment that anything comes into existence it is already out of existence, since time, like a flowing stream, sweeps all things along. But this faculty of the soul somehow or other lays hold of them and gives the shape and semblance of reality to what no longer exists in actuality. The oracle given to the Thessalians about Arne[61] instructed them to pay attention to

A deaf man's hearing, a blind man's sight.

But memory is for us both the hearing of the things to which we are deaf and the seeing of things to which we are blind. And so, as I said, there is nothing to be surprised at if, with its command over things which no longer exist, the soul also anticipates many things which have not yet come into existence. Such things in fact are closer to it and it is more nearly in time with them, since it is with the future that it is bound up and associated, and it has finished with all that is past and ended, except in so far as memory is concerned.

40. 'This power, then, is innate in the soul. It is dim, certainly, and imprecise in expression; yet it often happens that the soul will blossom out in its full radiance in dreams and sometimes in the hour of death. Then the body becomes cleansed and purified or else acquires just the right tem-

---

61. A Boeotian town, which the Thessalians are said to have captured sixty years after the Trojan war (Thucydides, I. 12).

perament to enable the reasoning and intelligent element in the soul to relax and to be freed from the pressure of the present as it wanders among the irrational and the fanciful areas of the future. Euripides says:

The best of prophets is the one who guesses well.[62]

But this is not true. The best prophet is the intelligent man who follows that element in the soul which is rational and which leads him along the lines of reasonable probability. But the faculty of forecasting the future is something essentially irrational and indeterminate; yet, like a tablet with no writing on it, it is capable of receiving impressions and presentiments coming to it from outside and, following no logical plan, it grasps at the future when it has withdrawn itself a long way from the present. And this withdrawal comes about through a peculiar physical condition caused by a change which we call "enthusiasm" or "inspiration". It often happens that the body can attain this state unaided and of its own accord. But men are also affected by streams of varying potency issuing from the earth. Some of these drive people crazy or cause disease or death; the effect of others is good, soothing and beneficial, as is clear from the experience of those who have come into contact with them. But the flow and breath of prophecy is the most divine and the holiest, whether it comes directly through the air or with the flow of a running stream. Entering into and mingling with the body, it produces in the soul a strange and unwonted condition, the precise nature of which is very hard to describe, although in many ways we may be helped by analogy. It is likely, for instance, that some kinds of passages for presentiment of the future are opened up by a diffusion of heat in much the same way as wine, when it rises to the head, will prompt move-

62. Fr. 973.

ments of the limbs which are out of the ordinary and bring into the open words and ideas till then latent and unexpressed.

For Bacchic rites
And minds in frenzy can produce much prophecy,

as Euripides[63] says. And this happens when the soul becomes heated and fiery and throws aside the caution and restraint which are imposed on it by human intelligence and often turn aside or stifle prophetic enthusiasm.

41. 'It is also quite reasonable to suppose that with the heat a dryness is also produced which refines the spirit and makes it ethereal and pure; for this is what Heraclitus calls "the dry soul".[64] Moisture not only dulls sight and hearing, but on the surface of mirrors and in combination with air will take away their brightness and their sheen. On the other hand it is quite possible that the explanation may be just the opposite of this; it may be that the prophetic element in the soul is tempered and made keen by a kind of chilling and contraction of the spirit, as in the case of steel when plunged into cold water. Or again, just as tin when alloyed with copper, which is soft and porous, holds and binds it together and at the same time makes it brighter and cleaner, so it is quite possible that the prophetic exhalation, which has some kind of fellowship and kinship with the soul, may by filling up and fitting itself into the empty spaces compact everything together. For one thing is appropriate and useful for one thing, another for another, just as when mixed with the dye beans are good for producing purple and sodium carbonate for producing scarlet, "splendour of shining scarlet mingled and held in the linen", as Empedocles[65] has it. And, my dear Demetrius, we have heard your account of the Cydnus and the sacred sword of Apollo in

63. *Bacchae*, 298.
64. Heraclitus, Fr. B. 118 ('A dry soul is best'), in H. Diels and W. Kranz (eds.), *Die Fragmente der Vorsokratiker*, 6th ed., Berlin, 1954.
65. Empedocles, fr. B. 93, ibid.

Tarsus: how the Cydnus will clean no steel except that sword, and how that sword can be cleaned by no other water but that of the Cydnus.

42. 'So there is nothing to be surprised at in the fact that, although the earth sends up many influences, only some of them have the power to produce the right condition in the soul for prophetic inspiration and visions of the future. My argument is undoubtedly supported by legends of the past. We hear, for instance, that the first occasion when the power that is in this place became manifest was when a shepherd fell down into it by accident and afterwards made a number of prophetic and inspired pronouncements. At first they were treated with contempt by the man's companions, a contempt which later turned to amazement, when what he had foretold actually came true. The most learned of the Delphians have preserved the tradition of this man's name; it was, they say, Coretas.

'But in my view what seems likeliest is that the soul has the same sort of close and intimate connexion with the prophetic spirit as the vision has with light, which is of like nature. The eye has the power to see, but it cannot perform its function without light; so, in the same way, the prophetic power of the soul, like the eye, needs the help of something kindred to it in order for it to be kindled and sharpened. Hence the general opinion of the past was that Apollo and the Sun are one and the same god; but those who could understand and respect the beauty and subtlety of analogy took this to mean that as body is to soul, as vision is to intellect, and light to truth, so is the power of the sun to the nature of Apollo; and they declared that the sun is the offspring and child of Apollo, eternally coming into existence as he eternally exists. The sun kindles and promotes and joins in the operation of the power of vision in our perception, and this is just what Apollo does for the power of prophecy in the soul.

43. 'It was natural, however, that those who held the view that the two are one and the same god should dedicate the oracle to Apollo and Earth in common, believing that the sun creates in the earth the right conditions and the right temperament for it to be able to produce the exhalations which inspire prophecy. Hesiod (who had a clearer understanding of things than some philosophers) addressed the Earth itself as:

> Sure foundation of all things,[66]

and we too believe it to be eternal and imperishable. But with regard to the powers that are associated with the earth, it is quite likely that these should change their locations, that their flow impelled from some other direction should alter its course and that within the earth there should be in the whole course of time many revolutions of such cyclical processes. Our own senses will provide many examples of this. Lakes, rivers, and even more frequently hot springs have in some places dwindled or completely disappeared and in others drained away, as it were, or sunk underground; later they have come back again, sometimes reappearing in the same place as before, sometimes rising to the surface again in another place near by. We know too that mines become exhausted; and in some cases this has happened quite recently, as with the silver mines in Attica and the copper ore in Euboea from which the cold-forged sword blades used to be made:

> And in his hand, self-sharpened, the Euboean sword,

as Aeschylus[67] says. And it was only recently that the quarries in Euboea ceased to produce in the rock formation those soft filaments looking like yarn. Some of you, I imagine, must have seen towels, nets, and women's head shawls from there. These cannot be burned in fire; in fact when any of them gets dirty through use, they throw them into the flames and then

66. *Theogony*, 117.   67. Aeschylus, fr. 356.

take them out all bright and shining. Today all this has gone and it is almost impossible to find any of these thin filaments, like hairs, running through the rock.

44. 'According to the school of Aristotle all these phenomena in the earth are brought about by exhalation and it is in accordance with exhalation that things of this kind neccessarily disappear, change from place to place, or again have their vigour renewed. And the same view should certainly be accepted with regard to the spirits of prophecy; their power should not be thought of as eternal and ageless, but as subject to change. Very heavy rainfall is likely to extinguish these exhalations, thunderbolts are likely to disrupt them, and particularly when there are earthquakes accompanied by subsidence and collapse deep down in the earth the exhalations will find different exits or no exit at all. Such a thing no doubt happened here, where they say that there are still traces of the great earthquake which actually destroyed the city. They say too that in Orchomenos there was an epidemic costing many lives and that the oracle of Teiresias there faded away altogether and today is still silent and voiceless. We have heard that much the same thing has happened to the oracles in Cilicia; but about this, Demetrius, you are the person who would best be able to inform us.'

45. 'I don't know the state of affairs there now,' said Demetrius. 'As you know, I've been abroad for a long time. But when I was there, both the oracle of Mopsus and the oracle of Amphilochus were still thriving. And I can tell you a most extraordinary thing which I found out when I was visiting the oracle of Mopsus. The ruler of Cilicia was himself still in two minds about religion, through lack of confidence, I imagine, in his own scepticism. Certainly in everything else he was arrogant and vulgar enough. He had at his court some Epicureans, men who are self-declared despisers of such things as oracles – no doubt because of their wonderfully scientific

understanding of the natural world. So he sent a freedman, like a spy into hostile territory, and arranged that he should have a sealed tablet inside which, unseen by anybody, his question was written. The man went and, as the custom is, spent the night in the sacred precinct where he went to sleep. In the morning he gave the following account of the dream which he had had. He dreamed that a very good-looking man had stood beside him and said one word, "black", and nothing else; he had then immediately vanished. We found this most extraordinary and very difficult to explain, but the ruler was absolutely astonished and he fell down on his face and worshipped the divinity. He opened the tablet and showed us the question that was written there. It was "Shall I sacrifice to you a white bull or a black one?" The result was that the Epicureans were utterly confounded and the ruler himself not only performed the sacrifice, but continued ever afterwards to revere Mopsus.'

46. During the silence that followed this story of Demetrius I felt impelled somehow to put as it were the final touches to our discussions, and I glanced again towards Philip and Ammonius, who were sitting next to each other. They seemed to be wanting to say something and so I contained myself. Then Ammonius said: 'Philip also has some comments to make, Lamprias, on what has been said. For he, like most people, thinks that Apollo and the sun are one and the same god. But my difficulty is a greater one and it concerns matters of more importance. I don't know quite how, but somehow or other we have been carried away by the force of our argument into taking away the prophetic power from the gods and transferring it to beings who are merely daimons. But now it looks as though we are proceeding to get rid of these daimons too and are driving them out from the oracle and the tripod here. We are attributing the origin of prophecy, or rather its very essence and power, to winds, to vapours, and

to exhalations. For these appropriate conditions of temperature and compression which we have been talking of have the effect of reducing even more the glory of the gods and must suggest some such a view of the first cause as that which Euripides puts into the mouth of his Cyclops:

> Earth of necessity, whether it wills it so or not,
> Brings forth the grass to fatten up my grazing flocks.[68]

Except that the Cyclops does not offer his flocks in sacrifice to the gods; instead he sacrifices them to himself and to his "stomach, the most important deity"; whereas we offer both sacrifices and prayers when we consult the oracles. But why on earth should we do this, if our souls contain the power of prophecy in themselves, a power which becomes operative because of some particular atmospheric condition? And what is the point of the ritual pouring of water over the victims? And why is it that no reply must be given unless the animal trembles and shudders all over from its hoofs to its head, when the water is poured over it? A mere tossing of the head as in other sacrifices is not enough; the animal must shiver and shake in all its limbs at once, and emit a quavering kind of cry. And if this does not happen, they declare that the oracle is not functioning and do not even bring in the prophetic priestess. Now it is reasonable to suppose that they act and believe like this because they consider that a god or a daimon is in the main responsible for the oracle. But according to you this is not a reasonable assumption. So long as this exhalation is there, the prophetic impulse, whether the animal trembles or not, will be aroused and it will affect the soul not only of the priestess, but of anyone else who happens to be there. It is therefore stupid to employ just one woman as a prophetess and to trouble her by having her watched to see that she keeps pure and chaste all through her life. For this man, Coretas, who

68. *Cyclops*, 332–3.

according to the Delphians fell down into the place and was the first to provide us with any knowledge of the power inherent in it, was not, I imagine, any different from all the rest of the goatherds and shepherds – that is if the whole story is not, as I think, a mere myth or a fabrication. In fact when I think of all the benefits which the Greeks have received from this oracle in war, in the founding of cities, in times of pestilence or of famine, it seems to me a monstrous thing to ascribe its discovery and origin to the mere accident of chance rather than to God and to Providence. And on this point,' he added, 'I should like to hear what Lamprias has to say, that is if Philip will be kind enough to wait.'

'I will, certainly,' said Philip, 'and so will all the others. We have all been very moved by what you have just said.'

47. I turned to him and said, 'I myself, Philip, have been not only moved but really upset at the idea that in front of all you good people I may have given the impression, so incongruous with my youth, of priding myself on a convincing piece of logic and of trying to destroy or undermine some religious belief which has been reached in a true and reverent spirit. I shall defend myself by calling on Plato to act as my witness and at the same time my counsel. Plato [69] found fault with the old philosopher Anaxagoras because he was too much concerned with physical causes and was always searching for and pursuing the laws of necessity as exemplified in the behaviour of physical bodies, while taking no account of the purpose and the agency behind their behaviour, which are better and higher first causes. Yet Plato also was the first, or the most thorough, of the philosophers in pursuing his investigations in both of these directions. On the one hand he made God the origin of all that is concerned with pure reason; but on the other hand he did not take away from matter the causes necessary for the process of coming into being; he

69. *Phaedo*, 96 ff.

realized that the perceptible universe, ordered as it is, is not pure and unalloyed, but comes into existence from matter where matter is in conjunction with reason. Look first at what happens in the case of artists, and let us begin with the famous stand for the mixing-bowl here which Herodotus[70] called the "bowl-carrier". As its material causes it had fire and steel and softening by fire and tempering by cold water, and without these the work could not possibly have been produced; but it was art and reason which constituted the more powerful causal principle, setting all these in motion and working through them. In fact the name of the author and creator of these likenesses and portraits is recorded in the inscription:

> Polygnotus, the son of Aglaophon, from Thasos,
> Painted here the sack of the high fortress of Troy;[71]

so he is evidently the artist. But no such composition as that which we see could possibly have come into being without the various pigments being ground together and mixed. But suppose a man wants to concentrate on the material cause and studies and teaches all about the properties of the red earth of Sinope and the light-coloured earth of Melos and the changes which they undergo when mixed with yellow ochre or with lamp-black, is he by so doing detracting from the reputation of the artist? Suppose he works in research on the hardening and softening of steel – how it loses its firmness in the fire and becomes malleable and pliant for those who forge and shape it; and then again, when plunged into clear water, how, because its texture had become loose and soft by the action of the fire, it takes on that well-tempered strength which Homer has described as "the might of steel"[72] – does he

70. *History*, 1. 25.

71. Simonides, fr. 160, in T. Bergk, *Poetae Lyrici Graeci*, 3rd ed., Leipzig, 1866.

72. *Odyssey*, 9. 393.

in any way neglect or underrate the artist's final responsibility for the creation of the work? I certainly do not think so. And there are also some people who dispute the value of various drugs used in medicine, but they leave the science of medicine intact. And so when Plato[73] asserted that vision comes from the rays from our eyes mingling with the light of the sun and that hearing comes from the vibrations of the air, he most certainly did not mean to deny the fact that it is in accordance with Reason and Providence that we have been gifted with sight and hearing.

48. 'To sum up then: there are, I maintain, two causes for everything in creation; but the poets and theologians of ancient times chose to give their attention only to the superior one of these causes and this was the well-known phrase which they applied to everything that exists:

Zeus the beginning and Zeus in the middle and all things are from Zeus.[74]

But in those days they had not yet gone on to consider the causality to be found in the laws of nature. Later generations of thinkers – those whom we call natural philosophers – do just the opposite; they have moved away from the beautiful and the divine in causality and ascribe everything to material bodies in their various interactions, mutations and combinations. And so the reasoning of both parties leaves something to be desired; there is ignorance of or lack of interest in the creator and the agent on the one side and of the material and the instrument on the other. Plato was the first to show a clear understanding and grasp of both aspects; to the rationally creative and dynamic force he added, as something necessary, the underlying matter which is acted upon; and his example

73. *Republic*, 507 C–D and 508 D.
74. A hymn to Zeus attributed to Orpheus: O. Kern, *Orphicorum Fragmenta*, pp. 90, 206, Berlin, 1922.

will clear us also of all suspicion of impiety. We do not deny the divinity and the rationality of prophecy when we attribute to it the composition of the soul of a human being, and, as its tool or plectrum, a state of enthusiasm and exhalations from the ground. In the first place, like our fathers before us we acknowledge the divinity of the earth, which gives rise to the exhalations, and of the sun, which gives the earth all its power of blending and transmuting substance. And in the second place, there does not appear to be anything unreasonable or impossible in our view that the daimons remain as overseers, ministers and guardians of this ordered system, keeping it, as it were, in tune, now slackening and now, at the appropriate time, increasing the tension, taking away from it what may be too disruptive, and disturbing to those under its influence and keeping its emotive force within the limits of what is painless and harmless. Nor is there anything contradictory to our argument in the fact that we offer preliminary sacrifices to find out the god's will and that we put garlands on the victims and pour libations over them. In offering the sacrifice and in pouring libations over the victim and observing how it moves and trembles, the priests and holy men declare that they have only one aim in view, which is to make sure that the god is present in his shrine. For what is to be offered in sacrifice must be pure, spotless and without blemish. So far as the body is concerned, it is not difficult to see whether these conditions are satisfied, but they also test the soul by putting meat before the bulls and peas before the boars, and they conclude that the animal that will not touch its food is of unsound mind. With goats the proof they use is cold water; for if the animal remains motionless and indifferent after being drenched in cold water, its soul cannot be in a normal state. And I cannot see how there would be anything to conflict with my argument even if it were positively proved that the trembling is a certain indication of the god's presence and that immobility would prove his absence. Every faculty expresses itself better or worse according to the particular occasion; and if we cannot tell exactly when the right occasion is, it is reasonable to suppose that the god will give us the necessary indications.

50. 'So I think that the exhalation is not always and in all circumstances constant; it will weaken and then again become stronger. And as evidence for this I can produce as witnesses all the ministers in attendance at the shrine and very many visitors as well. It does not happen often or regularly, but it does happen from time to time that the room in which they seat consultants of the oracle is filled with a fragrance and breath like the odour of the sweetest and richest perfumes, and this is wafted towards them as if arising from the inner recesses of the shrine. Probably this fragrance blossoms out as a result of heat or some other force present in the place. And if you find this difficult to believe, you will at least admit that the Pythian priestess herself, in that part of her soul with which the spirit of inspiration makes contact, is affected by influences of different kinds which vary from time to time, and that she does not always have exactly the same disposition, like a harmonious system which never alters. In fact she is often conscious, though more often unconscious, of various perturbations and disturbances which fasten on her body and make their way into her soul. And when she is under their power, it is better for her not to go into the shrine and put herself under the control of the god; for instead of being entirely free and untroubled, like a well-strung and well-tuned musical instrument, she will be in an emotional and unstable state. The drinker is not always affected by wine in exactly the same way, nor does the religious enthusiast get in the same state every time he hears the flute. In fact the same people feel the Bacchic emotion or are elated by the wine to a greater or a lesser degree according to changes in their inner

disposition at the particular time. And especially the imaginative element of the soul seems to change with and be controlled by changes which take place in the body. Dreams provide a clear example of this; sometimes our sleep is full of numbers of dreams of all kinds, and at other times they fade away into complete calm and tranquillity. We all know Cleon here, from Daulia, and he tells us that in all his long life he has never had a single dream; and among the older men the same thing is said of Thrasymedes of Heraea. The cause of this is the character or temperament of the body; so at the other extreme we find the melancholics, with a temperament that disposes them to all sorts of dreams and visions; and this is why their dreams are regarded as reliable, since with their fantasy operating in so many directions, like a man who shoots a lot of arrows, they often hit the target.

51. 'And so whenever the imaginative and prophetic faculty is properly adjusted to receive the spirit, as it might be a medicine, then the prophet will necessarily reach the state of ecstatic inspiration; and if these conditions are not fulfilled then inspiration will not come or, if it does, it will be misleading, impure and confused. We know this from the case of the Pythian prophetess who died not so long ago. This is what happened. A deputation from abroad had arrived to consult the oracle and, so they say, the sacrificial animal remained motionless and absolutely unaffected by the first libations poured over it. But the priests wanted to show what they could do; they persisted and went much too far and it was only when the animal was drenched and nearly drowned that it finally gave in. And now what happened to the prophetess? They say that she went down into the oracular chamber reluctantly and unwillingly; in the very first replies that she gave it was clear from the harshness of her voice that she was not responding as she should; she was like a ship in heavy seas and was filled with some dark and evil spirit.

Finally she lost all control and shrieking out some unintelligible words she rushed to the exit and threw herself down on the ground. It was so frightening that not only did the members of the deputation run away, but so did Nicander, the interpreter of the oracle, and other priests who were there. However, after a short time they went back and lifted her up. She was still conscious and lived on for a few days.

'It is because of this that they insist that the priestess's body must be pure from sexual intercourse and that her life must be uncontaminated by any contact with people outside and also that they take the omens before the oracle; for they think that it is clear to the god when she is in the right condition and with the right temperament to submit to the ecstasy of inspiration without harm to herself. For the power of the spirit does not affect everyone, or even the same person, always in the same way; what it provides is a spark and a starting point, as we have said, for those who are in the right state to feel the influences and undergo the change. The source of this power is indeed the gods and the daimons, but in spite of this it is not perpetual or imperishable or ageless, lasting into that infinite time under the load of which, according to our doctrine, all things between earth and moon are wearied out. Some people in fact maintain that the things above the moon are transitory too; in the face of the everlasting and the infinite, they fade away and are constantly suffering transmutations and rebirths.

52. 'And so,' I concluded, 'I recommend that you, and I too, should often give our attention to these subjects. Much, no doubt, has been said to which objections might be raised, and much might suggest different conclusions. But we cannot examine all these possibilities now. So let us postpone their discussion until later, and also the discussion of Philip's problem about the Sun and Apollo.'

The Cleverness of Animals, both of the Sea and of the Land

*   *
*

INTRODUCTORY NOTE

THE setting of this dialogue is in Plutarch's own circle. First, his father Autobulus goes over with a friend, Soclarus, the main points of a discussion supposed to have been held the previous day. This was about hunting and about the reasoning powers of animals. As a sequel, some young men have been preparing to debate the further question whether land animals or sea animals are more intelligent. They now produce their material, in a pair of set speeches. An older member of the party is to adjudicate.

In the first discussion, as often in Plutarch, an Academic and anti-Stoic thesis is presented. The young men's speeches are less theoretical: they constitute a sort of anthology of animal stories and odd facts of natural history, some of them very dubious, of a kind very popular in Roman times. Aelian's *History of Animals* uses much of the same material; indeed, Aelian evidently read Plutarch. But the original collections of such things were made by Aristotle and his successors. Where Plutarch excels is in the sympathy, elegance and vivacity with which he tells the stories.

CHARACTERS IN THE DIALOGUE

AUTOBULUS: Plutarch's father.
SOCLARUS: an old friend.
OPTATUS: an elderly man.

97

ARISTOTIMUS,

PHAEDIMUS,   young students.

HERACLEON:

1. AUTOBULUS: Leonidas was once asked what he
thought of Tyrtaeus. He replied 'a good poet, for sharpening the souls of the young', and he meant by this that the
poetry of Tyrtaeus makes young men eager for action and
gives them a vitality and a sense of ambition so that they will
not spare themselves in battle. And now, my friends, I am
much afraid that the *Praise of Hunting*, which we had read to
us yesterday, may have rather too strong an effect on the
young men among us who are fond of hunting and may lead
them to give themselves over entirely to this pursuit and to
think of all other subjects as being either of secondary importance or altogether meaningless. I must own that I myself, in
spite of my age, found myself fired all over again and longing,
like Phaedra in Euripides:

> To shout to the hounds, chasing the dappled deer,[1]

so deeply was I affected by what was said and by the solid
convincing arguments brought forward.

SOCLARUS: I quite agree with you, Autobulus. That
reader we had yesterday seemed to be rousing his eloquence
from a long sleep to give pleasure to the young men and to
join with them in celebrating the spring. I was particularly
pleased with the way he brought in the subject of gladiators
and showed that one of the important reasons for being
enthusiastic about hunting is that it takes over, as it were,
most of that pleasure, whether natural or acquired, that we
find in watching armed combats between human beings, and
gives us a pure pleasure in the spectacle of a contest between
skill and intelligent courage on the one hand and brute

1. cf. *Hippolytus*, 218 f.

strength and violence on the other. It supports that passage
in Euripides:

> Man's strength is small and yet
> In the turns of his subtle mind
> He masters the monstrous brood
> Of the sea and the beasts
> Of the air and the earth.[2]

2. AUTOBULUS: And yet, my dear Soclarus, there is a view
which holds that men became insensitive and savage because
of the taste for bloodshed they acquired in hunting; instead
of being disgusted by the blood and the wounds of animals
they learnt actually to take pleasure in their slaughter. Things
then went on as happened in Athens at the time of the Thirty.[3]
The first man put to death by them was an informer who was
said to deserve it; so was the second and the third. But after
that they began to go further and further, making away with
men who had nothing against them; and in the end they did
not spare even the very best of the citizens. So the first man
to kill a bear or a wolf was honoured for it; and it may be
that a cow or a pig was thought to have deserved slaughter
because it had tasted the sacred offerings that were put in front
of it. Deers, hares and antelopes were the next to be eaten and
then men turned to their first taste of the flesh of sheep and,
in some places, of dogs and horses.

> The tame goose and the dove within the household,

as Sophocles[4] says, were torn limb from limb and carved up
for food; and men did not do this under the compulsion of
hunger, as cats and weasels do, but simply for the pleasure of
an appetizing taste. And so what is brutish and bloodthirsty

2. Fr. 27 (from *Aeolus*).
3. The oligarchic government which ruled Athens for a short time
after the defeat by the Spartans in A.D. 404.
4. Fr. 782.

in human nature was reinforced and made insensitive to pity, while the elements of kindness and gentleness lost most of their keenness. Acting on the contrary principle, the Pythagoreans, in order to promote loving kindness and compassion among men, were particularly careful to be kind to animals. For consistent regular behaviour is extraordinarily powerful, gradually infiltrating into the emotions and making men better.

But I see that, without noticing it, we have somehow got into a discussion which has a bearing not only on our conversations yesterday, but also on the argument which is going to take place today. Yesterday, you will remember, we put forward the view that all animals show, in one way or another, reason and intelligence and we suggested to our young friends who like hunting a most educative and very enjoyable subject to debate, namely the question whether land animals or sea animals are the cleverer. And we shall judge this debate today, I think – that is, if the parties of Aristotimus and of Phaedimus stand by their challenges. Aristotimus promised his friends that he would maintain that the land produces the most intelligent animals, and Phaedimus was to speak in favour of the animals of the sea.

SOCLARUS: They'll stick by what they said, Autobulus; and they should be here any minute now. I saw them early this morning and they were both getting ready for the contest. But before it starts, do you mind if we look over some points which have to do with our conversation yesterday but were either not discussed, because there was not time, or were not treated very seriously because we were enjoying our wine? I kept hearing in my ears the sound of some very material objections that might be raised against us by the Stoics. Would they not say that, just as the immortal is opposed to the mortal, the imperishable to the perishable or, indeed, the incorporeal to the corporeal, so, if the rational exists, there must necessarily exist the irrational as an opposite and a counterpart? In the whole list of opposites going with each other we cannot leave just this one incomplete and standing on one leg.

3. AUTOBULUS: But, my dear Soclarus, has anyone ever maintained that, while the rational in things exists, the irrational does not? There is all the irrational you can want in all things that do not have a soul and we need no other kind of antithesis to the rational. Obviously everything that does not have a soul is without reason and intelligence and is in opposition to what has a soul and also has reason and understanding. If, to make sure that nature is not curtailed in any way, someone maintains that the part of nature which has a soul must comprise both a rational and an irrational element, then someone else is sure to say that what has a soul must comprise elements capable of imagination and incapable of imagination, capable of feeling and incapable of feeling. The idea would be that these opposites, these positive and negative antitheses about the same thing should be kept, as it were, in equilibrium. But when we consider that all things which have souls must necessarily be capable of feeling and of imagination, it will appear absurd to go looking in this class of living things, for antitheses between the feeling and the unfeeling, the imaginative and the unimaginative. And in just the same way it is pointless to find in living things an antithesis between the rational and the irrational – especially when the argument is addressed to men who believe that all things which are capable of feeling are also capable of intelligence, and that every living thing is provided by nature with reason and the power of forming an opinion just as it is provided with sensation and appetite.

These philosophers say rightly that nature does nothing without a purpose and without an end in view; and nature did not give creatures sensation simply so that they should be aware of something happening to them. The fact is that in the creature's environment there is much that is friendly and much that is hostile, and no creature could survive for a moment if it had not learnt to keep away from what is dangerous and to go after what is good for it. Certainly it is by sensation that a creature is able to recognize the difference; but what follows upon sensation – the capture or pursuit of what is beneficial and the avoidance of or running away from what is dangerous or painful – could not possibly occur in creatures which were not endowed by nature with some degree of reason, discrimination, memory and concentration. Suppose you took away from a creature all expectation, memory, design and thought for the future, all hope, fear, desire, distress; such a creature would have no use for eyes or ears either, even though it had them. If one cannot make use of sensation and imagination, it would be better to be rid of them all together rather than to feel suffering and pain and distress without having any means at all of escaping from them.

In fact there is a work of Strato,[5] the natural scientist, which shows that sensation itself is quite impossible without some action of the mind. It is true that when our attention is elsewhere, the letters on a page may fall on our eyes or the sounds of speech on our ears without our grasping their meaning; but soon the mind comes to itself and gets back on to its track and picks up everything that had been overlooked; and this is what is meant by the saying: 'In the mind is sight and hearing; all the rest is deaf and blind', so showing that without the presence of the mind visual and auditory impressions do not result in perception. As in the case of King Cleomenes[6]

5. Of Lampsacus, successor of Theophrastus as head of the Lyceum, d. 272 B.C. The line of Epicharmus quoted just below seems to have been used by Strato himself.

6. Presumably Cleomenes III of Sparta, whose life Plutarch wrote.

who, after a performance at a banquet had been loudly applauded, was asked whether he did not think it excellent and replied 'That is for the rest of you to decide. My mind is in the Peloponnese.' So, if it is a law of nature that to have sensation we must have intelligence, it must necessarily follow that all creatures which have sensation must also have intelligence.

Suppose we assume that sensation does not require intelligence in order to carry out its proper function; all the same, when the operation of sensation has enabled the animal to tell the difference between what is friendly and what is dangerous, we must ask what it is that from that time on remembers the distinction and fears what will cause pain and desires what will do good. And what is it in animals that, if what it wants is not there, will work out means of getting hold of it and will build lairs and hiding places which can be used either as traps or ambushes or as places of refuge? And yet in their 'elementary introductions' these authors[7] are constantly dinning into our ears their definitions of 'purpose' as 'signification of desire for completion', 'design' as 'impulse preceding another impulse', 'preparation' as 'action preceding another action' and 'memory' as 'apprehension of a proposition in the past which has been approved by sensation in the present'.[8] Every one of these is a term used in logic; and all of them apply to the behaviour of all animals. So too does everything they say about cognition which, when inactive, is described by them as 'notional' and, when put into action, as 'conceptual'. They admit that all emotions without distinction are 'improper judgements based on opinion'; but I am amazed that they fail altogether to notice that many of the actions and movements of animals show anger and fear

7. The Stoics.
8. That is, sensation gives us the proposition 'this is dangerous', memory the proposition 'this was dangerous'.

and even, as I am quite sure, envy or jealousy. And they themselves do not punish dogs and horses for their mistakes for no reason at all; they do it in order to teach them how to behave; by inflicting pain on them they are implanting in them a feeling of regret or what, in the case of ourselves, we call repentance.

Pleasure received through hearing is a kind of enchantment and the pleasure that comes through the eyes is a kind of magic. Both are used against animals. Deer and horses are enchanted by the sound of pipes and flutes, and crabs cannot resist the impulse to come out of their holes when they hear lotus pipes. I have heard too that shad will come up to the surface and be attracted towards the noise of singing and clapping hands. And then there is the long-eared owl which can be caught when under the influence of the magic of seeing people dancing in front of him; he becomes so delighted that he tries to wriggle his shoulders to the rhythm of the dance.

There are some people who, instead of admitting that animals feel pleasure or anger or fear or plan for the future or have memory, will use a feeble locution and say that the bee behaves 'as if' it had memory, the swallow 'as if' it were planning a nest for the future, the lion 'as if' it were angry, the deer 'as if' it were afraid. I wonder how they would react if one were to say that animals do not see or hear but behave 'as if' they could; that they make no sound but behave 'as if' this was what they did; that, indeed, they are not alive but look 'as if' they were. For so far as I can see these last statements are no more contrary to plain evidence than are the statements they make.

4. SOCLARUS. Well, Autobulus, so far as all this goes you can certainly count me in on your side. All the same, when I compare the behaviour of animals with the customs and lives and actions and general conduct of human beings, I find that animals are inferior in many ways and particularly in one

way: there is no evidence at all that they pursue virtue, and it is for the pursuit of virtue that reason exists; they make no progress towards virtue and they show no appetite for it; and I am at a loss to understand how Nature can have given the ability to take the first step to creatures who are incapable of reaching its goal.

AUTOBULUS: As to this point, Soclarus, even these opponents of ours do not appear to find anything strange about it. They will maintain that love of one's offspring is the foundation of the community and of justice among human beings and they will observe that among animals this love is often found in a highly developed form; and yet they will still confidently assert that animals can have no notion of justice.

Now take the case of mules: they have all the organs for reproduction; they have wombs and genitals and they take pleasure in using them; and yet they are incapable of reaching the final end by reproduction. Or look at it this way: it would be absurd to pretend that people like Socrates or Plato are involved in just as much vice as the commonest slave and are equally foolish and intemperate and unjust; is it not just as absurd to point to what is impure and imperfectly formed in the virtue of animals and to account for it by saying not that their reason is undeveloped and weak, but that they have no reason at all? And it is particularly absurd coming from people who admit that vice is a fault of reason and that animals are full of vice. For we do in fact see among animals many examples of cowardice and intemperance and injustice and malice.

If one is going to say that creatures which are not equipped by nature to allow of the full development of reason have therefore no reasoning powers at all, one might just as well say that apes are not naturally ugly or tortoises not naturally slow because the former have no capacity for beauty or the latter for speed. And in the second place one would be blind to a distinction which is quite obvious: reason in itself is the gift of nature, but the strengthening and the perfection of reason comes from cultivation and education. All living creatures, therefore, have the faculty of reason; but if what one is looking for is truth and perfect wisdom, then not even man can be said to possess that. There is a difference between the way a hawk and a cicada uses its vision, and the way an eagle or a partridge flies, and just as there are these differences in sight and in flight, so every creature that is gifted with reason has not the same accuracy and dexterity in the use of it. Among animals we can find many examples of social feeling and courage and enterprise and providence; but the opposite qualities are also to be found – injustice, cowardice and stupidity. In fact the controversy among our young men which is to take place today bears witness to this; for the two sides are assuming that the difference exists, when one party maintains that land animals and the other that sea animals are by nature the more advanced in virtue. This is clear too if you contrast hippopotami with storks. Storks look after their fathers and feed them, but hippopotami kill their fathers so that they can mate with their mothers. Or compare doves with partridges. The cock partridge, because the hen will not mate when she is sitting, steals the eggs and destroys them; but male doves actually help in looking after the nest and take their turn in keeping the eggs warm and are the first to feed the fledglings; and if the female is away too long, the male will peck her with his beak and force her to go back to the eggs or to the young birds.

Antipater[9] attacks donkeys and sheep for their dirty habits. Why did he have nothing to say about lynxes and swallows? Lynxes carry away their excrement and bury it, and swallows

9. Probably Antipater of Tarsus, a Stoic philosopher of the second century B.C.

teach their young to turn round and let their droppings fall outside the nest.

Why is it that we can say that a dog is more intelligent than a sheep, or that a stag is more cowardly than a lion, but we do not say that one tree is more intelligent than another tree or that one vegetable is more cowardly than another one? The reason, surely, is that just as if we are talking of things which cannot move at all we cannot say that one is slower than another, or if we are talking of things that make no sound at all we cannot say that one is quieter than another, so with all creatures to whom Nature has not given the faculty of understanding it is impossible to make any distinctions between more or less cowardly or lazy or intemperate. It is only where reason is present, varying in kind and degree from one animal to another, that observable differences are to be detected.

5. SOCLARUS: Yet what an amazing difference there is between man and the animals in his ability to learn, his keenness of intellect and in all that concerns the claims of justice and life in a community.

AUTOBULUS: No doubt, my friend. There are also many animals greatly superior to all men in size, in speed, in keen sight and in sharp hearing; but this does not mean that man is blind or unable to move or deaf. We cannot run as fast as a deer, but we can still run; we can see, though not so well as a hawk; and Nature has not deprived us of all strength and magnitude even though, compared with elephants and camels, our strength and size are pretty inconsiderable. So, even if the understanding of animals is not so good as ours and their intellect is less efficient, we must not say that they have no understanding or intelligence at all. What we should say is that their intellect is weak and confused, like an eye that is misted over and out of focus. And if it were not for the fact that any moment now I am expecting our bright and learned young men to be here with their contributions – examples in plenty taken from the land and from the sea – I should not be able to stop myself from giving you thousands of examples of how animals can learn and how they show a natural goodness of disposition. One could go on drawing bucketful after bucketful of illustrations just from the imperial spectacles shown in the splendid city of Rome. However, we had better leave this subject fresh and untouched for them to exercise their abilities upon.

There is, however, one small point which I should like to discuss with you quietly. In my view each part and each faculty has a weakness or defect or disease which is peculiar to itself and not found anywhere else – blindness in the eye, for example, lameness in the legs, or stammering in the tongue. For in an organ which was not created to see there can be no blindness, nor can there be lameness in a part that was not created for walking; nor could you use the word 'stammering' of a creature without a tongue, or 'inarticulate' of one that was naturally incapable of making a sound. And in the same way you could not describe as delirious or crazy or mad anything which was by nature without reason or intelligence or understanding. For it is impossible to suffer a deficiency in a faculty or its total loss or any injury to it unless you possess this faculty in the first place. But you have certainly come across mad dogs and I myself have known of mad horses; and I have heard that cattle and foxes also go mad. However, the example of dogs will do. No one disputes the fact that dogs go mad and this provides evidence that this creature is a rational animal with considerable powers of understanding which, when they are disturbed and confused, will result in what we call rabies or madness. In this condition we can observe no impairment of vision or of hearing; and just as in the case of human beings who suffer from melancholy or insanity it is absurd not to admit that the damage or derangement is in the thinking or reasoning faculty (in fact the expressions we normally use of madmen are 'they are not themselves' or 'they are out of their minds'), so it is impossible to maintain that there is anything else wrong with mad dogs except a derangement of their natural powers of judgement, reason and memory, which become all confused with the result that the animals go mad and cannot recognize the faces of their friends and run away from the places they know best. Anyone who attributes their madness to any other reason must either be disregarding the evidence of his eyes or, if he sees where it leads, is just refusing to admit the truth.

6. SOCLARUS: I think that you have every right for that suspicion. Certainly we find the Stoics and the Peripatetics arguing very determinedly on the other side. According to them justice could never come into existence, but would remain entirely without form or substance, if all animals had reason. Either, they say, we must be guilty of injustice in taking their lives; or else, if we do not use them for food, all life will become impossible; once we stop using animals for food, we shall be forced in a way to live like animals ourselves. And I need not mention the vast numbers of Nomads and Troglodytes who know of no other food except the flesh of animals. But what about us, who like to think of ourselves as civilized humane people? It's hard to say what activities and arts on land or sea or in the air will be left to us or what will happen to our whole way of life, if we have to learn to be kind and considerate to all living creatures; and this is what we must be if they are gifted with reason and of the same kind as ourselves. We are left with the inescapable dilemma, either to do away with life or to do away with justice. And the only remedy, the only cure for this situation is to abide by that ancient and established definition by which, according to Hesiod,[10] he who separated the various classes

10. *Works and Days,* 277–9.

of creatures laid down the rule by which each should deal
with each:

> Fish, wild beasts and winged birds are free to eat one another:
> They have no notion of right. Right is known only to men.

It is impossible for us to be unjust to creatures who are incapable of acting rightly towards us. Reject this argument and
you leave no way, broad or narrow, by which justice may
get in.

7. AUTOBULUS: That speech of yours, my friend, was
certainly 'one from the heart'.[11] I think that these philosophers
should certainly not be allowed, as though they were women
having a difficult childbirth, to put a charm round their necks
to ensure quick delivery and so bring out into the world pain-
lessly and without trouble their idea of justice for us to see.
They themselves will not allow Epicurus,[12] when he is
arguing on subjects of the greatest importance, so slight, and
inconsiderable an assumption that one simple atom may make
the slightest deviation from its course – an assumption which
would enable him to show that the stars and living creatures
were created by chance and to account for free will in us.
What they tell him is that he must prove anything that is not
obvious. How, then, can they make the irrationality of
animals the basis for their own views on justice? It is a hypo-
thesis that is neither generally admitted by others nor demonstrated by them. We have, in fact, another way to justice and
it is a way that is not so slippery or so steep and does not lead
us through the denial of the obvious. Here Plato is the guide
and my son,[13] who is also your friend, Soclarus, points it out
to those who want just to follow and to learn instead of indulging in contentious arguments. Empedocles and Heraclitus

11. cf. Euripides, fr. 412.

12. Epicurus' 'swerve' of atoms was a notoriously vulnerable part of
his theory. See e.g. Lucretius, 2. 216 ff.

13. Plutarch himself.

certainly do not accept as true the view that man, treating animals as he does, is entirely free from injustice; their complaints and reproaches against Nature occur constantly – that she is 'Necessity' or 'Strife', that she contains nothing pure and unalloyed, but operates through all kinds of suffering and injustice. Birth itself, they say, is an example of this and must involve injustice, since it is a union of the mortal with the immortal and what is born is nourished unnaturally on parts of the body torn from the parent.

This, I agree, is strong language to use and seems to us rather too strong. For there is a calmer and more moderate approach which will allow animals to have reason and will also permit men, who make use of them as they should, to retain justice. This was the way of looking at things established by wise men in ancient times, but then gluttony and luxury combined together against it and drove it out of existence. But it was re-introduced by Pythagoras, who taught us how we can do good to ourselves without injustice. Animals which are savage and positively dangerous can be punished and killed without injustice while at the same time we tame those animals which are gentle and friendly to man and enlist their help in whatever work each has been naturally equipped for. Prometheus, in Aeschylus' play,[14] speaks of:

> The colts of horse and ass and progeny of bulls

and says that he gave them to us,

> To act as servants and to help us in our toil.

And so we use dogs to keep watch for us and we keep sheep and goats for their milk and their wool or hair. We are in no danger of extinction and life still goes on when men have no plates of fish for their banquets, no *pâté de foie gras*, no finely

14. *Prometheus Unbound*, fr. 194.

minced beef or flesh of kids. And life would still go on if we did not, sitting at our ease at the games or enjoying ourselves in the hunting field, force animals against their will to fight back against us or slaughter animals which lack the instinct to fight back even in self-defence. In my view true enjoyment of sport must mean that there is happiness on both sides – not the sort of thing of which Bion spoke when he said that boys throw stones at frogs for fun, but the frogs died not for fun at all, but in earnest. And in the same way men in hunting and fishing take pleasure in the sufferings and the death of animals and even in tearing them away most pitilessly from their cubs and nestlings. No, the injustice is not in making use of animals, but in making use of them wrongly and thoughtlessly and cruelly.

8. SOCLARUS: Autobulus, you must restrain yourself. No more accusations now! Quite a number of our friends are just coming and they are all keen hunters. You'll find it difficult to convert them and there's no need to hurt their feelings.

AUTOBULUS: Quite right. But I know Eubiotos well and my cousin Ariston and Aeacides and Aristotimus too, the sons of Dionysius of Delphi and Nicander, the son of Euthydamus – all of them to use Homer's[15] expression, 'most cunning' in the hunting field, and so they will be on Aristotimus' side. And here too comes Phaedimus, bringing with him his friends from the islands and from the sea coast, Heracleon from Megara and Philostratus from Euboea, 'hearts set on the works of the sea'.[16] And here comes Optatus, who is about my age. He is like Diomedes –

Hard it would be to tell with which of the armies he ranges.[17]

15. Perhaps Plutarch is thinking of *Odyssey*, 8. 159.
16. cf. Homer, *Iliad*, 2. 614; *Odyssey*, 5. 67.
17. Homer, *Iliad*, 5. 85.

He has given glory to the goddess who is both the Huntress and Dictynna by

> Many trophies hung before the shrine
> From sea and the hunt in the mountains.[17a]

It looks as though he's coming to join us and is not going to give his support to either side. Or am I wrong, my dear Optatus, in thinking that you are going to act as a fair and impartial umpire between the young men?

OPTATUS: No, you are quite right, Autobulus. There used to be an old law of Solon's, penalizing those who would not take either side in a dispute; but that law has long been obsolete.

AUTOBULUS: Then come and sit here with us, so that, if we need evidence we shall not have to look it all up in Aristotle, but will have your expert opinion to follow and so give a true verdict on the arguments we are to hear.

SOCLARUS: Now, young man, have you come to any agreement about how we are to proceed?

PHAEDIMUS: Yes, we have, Soclarus, though there was a good deal of disagreement first. In the end what Euripides[18] calls

> The lot, the child of chance

was brought in and now calls into court the case of the land animals first and the case of the animals of the sea afterwards.

SOCLARUS: Then, Aristotimus, the time has come for you to speak and for us to listen to you.

9. ARISTOTIMUS: The court is open. . . .[19] And there are

17a. Poetical quotation of unknown origin.
18. Fr. 989.
19. Here there is a lacuna, presumably a long one, though not marked in the MSS. The drift of the sentence that breaks off seems to be to draw a comparison or contrast between legal proceedings and the situation of the contestants in the dialogue.

some fish which waste their sperm by chasing the female while she is laying her eggs.

There is also a variety of the mullet, called the greyfish, which feeds on its own slime; and the octopus is so lazy, or so insensitive or so gluttonous, or all three at once, that he sits all through the winter feeding on himself,

Housed without light or heat, dwelling in difficult places.[20]

Here then is another reason why Plato in his *Laws*[21] not only forbade but begged and prayed that the young men should not 'be swept away by a passion for sea fishing'. No courage has to be practised, no skill has to be developed, not anything at all which exercises one's strength or quickness of movement or response when one is faced with bass or congers or parrot fish. But when the hunting is done on land then the animals with spirit and daring will develop in those who challenge them the qualities of courage and fearlessness; cunning animals will develop sharp wits and skill in their attackers and swift-footed animals will make their pursuers hardy and tough. This is why hunting is a noble sport, whereas there is no glory to be won in fishing. Can you point out any god, my friend, who has deigned to be called the 'conger-killer' as Apollo is called the 'wolf-killer', or 'mullet-slayer' as Artemis is called 'deer-slayer'? And no wonder, when it's a more glorious thing for a man to have caught and killed a wild boar or a stag or, for that matter, a gazelle or a hare, than to have bought one in the market. But as for tunnies and mackerel and bonitos, it's more creditable to pay money for them than to catch them oneself. They are such spiritless, hopeless, incapable creatures that they make the very idea of hunting them something disgusting and sordid and un-gentlemanly.

20. Hesiod, *Works and Days*, 524.
21. Laws, 823 D–E.

10. In general the evidence which philosophers adduce to show that animals have reason is as follows: they have purpose, they plan for the future, they have memory, they feel emotion, they care for their young and they show gratitude when they are treated well and hostility towards what hurts them; they can also look for and find what they need, and their behaviour can show positive goodness – courage, for example, a feeling for the community, self-restraint and magnanimity. Now let us ask ourselves whether there is any trace at all of these qualities in sea animals, or anything more than an exceedingly remote suggestion of them, so hard to discover that the observer can only just conjecture that it may be there. But in the case of animals which are born and go about on the land it is perfectly easy to find and to observe clear and undeniable examples of all the qualities I have mentioned.

Consider first of all the evidence of purpose and planning for the future shown by bulls churning up the dust before a fight and wild boars sharpening their tusks. Elephants' tusks get blunted and worn down by the digging up or felling of the trees on which they feed; and so they only use one tusk for this and keep the other one always sharp and pointed for defence. The lion always walks with his paws clenched and the claws drawn back so that their points may not be worn away and blunted and may not leave a clear spoor for the trackers. In fact it is very difficult to find a trace of the print of a lion's claw; the marks one finds are so slight and indistinct that one soon misses them and loses the trail.

And no doubt you've heard of how the ichneumon arms itself for battle with all the care of an infantry-man and how, when it is going to attack the crocodile, it plasters its body with a thick corselet of mud. And we have all seen how swallows prepare for the breeding season, how carefully they place the tougher twigs at the bottom of the nest as a foundation and then interweave the lighter ones; and if they see that the nest needs some mud to hold it together, they skim over the surface of a pond or stretch of sea, just touching the water with their feathers so as to moisten them but not to make them so wet as to weigh them down; and then they scoop up dust and in this dust-bath they make the mud firm and of the right consistency. And when their nest is finished, instead of having many angles and sides it is made as smooth and rounded as can be, secure and roomy and just the right shape to make it difficult for hostile creatures to reach from outside.

And there are many things to be admired in the spider's web, which is the model both for the looms used by women and for the nets used in fishing and hunting. How fine the thread is and how smooth the weaving! There are no joins to be seen and nothing like a warp; it is like a continuous thin membrane and has a tenacity which comes from some kind of sticky substance invisibly worked into the fabric. And then there is the blending of the colours, giving it the appearance of part of the air or mist and designed to make it inconspicuous. But most remarkable of all is the skill, comparable to that of a charioteer or a helmsman, with which the spider handles her device. When a victim is entangled, she is aware of it and, like a skilled huntsman with a net, is careful to close the trap at once and make it tight. We see this every day with our own eyes and so no one will dispute what I am saying. Otherwise it would seem a mere fairy story, as I myself once thought was the case with the story of the crows in Libya which, when they are thirsty, drop stones into a pot to fill it and raise the level of the water till it is within their reach. Later, however, I saw a dog on board ship, when the sailors were away, putting pebbles into a half-empty jar of olive oil and I was amazed at its intelligence in understanding that lighter substances are forced upwards as heavier substances settle to the bottom.

Other examples of the same sort of thing can be found in

the bees in Crete and in the geese in Cilicia. When the bees are about to take off for flight around a windy headland, they pick up tiny stones as ballast so as not to be carried out to sea. And when the geese fly over Mount Taurus, because of their fear of eagles they take a large stone in their beaks as a kind of gag or bridle on their natural tendency to honking and gaggling, so that they may get across the mountains in silence and unobserved.

The behaviour of cranes in flight is well known too. In high winds and rough weather they do not fly in line abreast or in a curving crescent, as they do on fine days; instead they at once adopt a wedge formation with the point cleaving through the wind as it streams past so that there will be no break in their ranks. And when they settle on the ground the birds that are to stand watch at night support themselves on one foot and grasp a stone in the other and hold on to it tightly. The necessary tension in the muscles will keep them awake for a long time and if they do relax, the fall of the stone will wake up the bird that has dropped it. This reminds me of Heracles with his bow tucked under his arm.

> With mighty arm enfolding it he takes his sleep
> And in his right hand still he firmly grips the club.[22]

Nor am I surprised at the man who first thought of how to open an oyster,[23] when I read of the ingenuity of herons. These birds will swallow a closed mussel and put up with the discomfort following until they realize that the shell has been softened and loosened by the heat in their bodies; they then disgorge the mussel all open and ready to eat and take out the edible part.

11. The social organization of ants and their planning for the future cannot possibly be dealt with in full detail, but they

22. From an unknown tragedian: *adespota*, fr. 416.
23. By putting it in hot water.

are too important to be passed over entirely. Nowhere else
has Nature provided something so small as a mirror for
greater and nobler things. Here you will find, as in a drop of
clear water, the reflection of every virtue,

> Love and good feeling are here,[24]

in their social organization. Courage too is reflected in their
ability to endure toil and hardship. There are also the elements
of self-control and many indications of prudence and justice.
Cleanthes denied that animals are rational; and yet he relates
the following experience: he saw some ants coming to a
strange ant-hill and carrying a dead ant with them. Other ants
then came out of the hill and held a kind of meeting with the
first party and then went back inside. This happened two or
three times until finally they brought up a grub as ransom
for the dead body. The first party then picked up the grub,
gave back the corpse and went away.

Among other things that everyone has noticed is the
considerate behaviour shown by ants when they meet; those
with no load to carry always give way to those who have a
load and allow them to pass first. And there is the way in
which they gnaw through and take to pieces burdens that are
hard to carry or difficult to get along so that with more ants
to help they will be easily transportable. And according to
Aratus[25] it is a sign of rain on the way when they spread out
their eggs and let them cool in the open air:

> When from their hollow nests the ants come hurrying upwards
> Carrying their eggs.

Though here some read *eia* (provisions) instead of *oia* (eggs)
as meaning their store of grain which they bring up to
surface when they see that it is getting mildewed and fear

24. Homer, *Iliad*, 14. 216.
25. *Phaenomena*, 956, cf. Vergil, *Georgics*, 1. 379 f.

that it may rot away and spoil. But the supreme example of their intelligence is to be found in their knowing in advance the moment when wheat will germinate. As you know, wheat does not remain dry and hard; in the process of germination it expands and becomes milky in texture. And so, to prevent it running to seed and losing its value as food and to keep it in an edible form, the ants eat out the germ from which the new wheat comes.

I do not approve of cutting ant-hills into sections, as it were anatomically, in order to learn more about them. However, those who do this tell us that the passage leading down into the ground is winding and difficult for any other creature to follow; it twists and turns and there are tunnels leading off from it with connecting galleries and it ends in three hollow chambers. One of these is for their general living quarters, another is a store room for their food and in the third they put the bodies of the dying.

12. You will agree, I imagine, that it is quite in order if I go directly on from ants to elephants. In this way we shall be able to consider the nature of intelligence in the smallest of animals and in the largest at the same time and to see that there are no signs of its fading away in the smallest creatures and no deficiency of it in the largest.

Now many people are astonished at all the things that elephants can learn or be taught in the way of taking up different postures and going through different movements for display in the circuses. And indeed their tricks are so various and so difficult to memorize and retain that even human beings would not find it at all easy to master them. I myself, however, find that this animal's understanding is more clearly displayed in a pure and undiluted state, that is to say in the movements and the feelings which are its own and have not been taught to it by others.

There is a case which happened not long ago in Rome. A

number of elephants were being trained in difficult balancing acts and in wheeling around in complicated patterns and one of them, who was the slowest to learn, was constantly being cursed at, and often punished. Now this beast was seen at night all by himself in the moonlight rehearsing what he had learnt and practising the exercises.

There was an elephant once in Syria, so Hagnon[26] tells us, which was fed in its owner's house, and every day the keeper, after he had received a measure of barley, made off with half of it for his own use. Once, however, when his master was there and looking on, the keeper poured out the full ration for the elephant, who took a look at it, raised up his trunk and separated the barley into two equal heaps, thus indicating in the clearest way possible how he had been cheated by the keeper. And there was another elephant whose keeper used to mix stones and earth in with his barley; this elephant scooped up some ashes and threw them into the pot where the keeper's meat was cooking. And there was another one in Rome who was being tormented by some small boys who were sticking their writing styluses into its trunk. The elephant seized hold of one of the boys, raised him high into the air and seemed about to hurl him to the ground; everyone near by cried out, but the elephant gently put the boy down again and went on his way, thinking that for a boy of that age a good fright was punishment enough.

As for elephants living on their own in the wild there are a number of amazing stories. None is more remarkable than what they do in fording rivers. The youngest and the smallest comes forward as a volunteer and goes in first while the others stand and watch, knowing that so long as the water does not reach the level of his back, the bigger elephants can have complete confidence in getting across safely.

26. Hagnon of Tarsus, Academic philosopher of the second century B.C.

13. Similar behaviour is to be observed in the fox and I must not forget to mention him at this point. Now according to the fables,[27] Deucalion released a dove from the ark knowing that if she came back inside it would be a sign that the storm was still raging, but that if she flew away it would show that fair weather was coming again. And at the present day the Thracians, when they want to cross a frozen river, use a fox to test the solidity of the ice. The fox goes slowly forward and lays its ear to the ice; if it perceives by the sound that there is running water close underneath, it will conclude that the ice has not solidified to any depth and it will stand still and, if they let it, come back on shore again. But if no sound is to be heard, it will take heart and go across. And we should not attribute this simply to keen perception unaided by reason. In fact the fox has argued from perception in a syllogism of this form: what makes noise must be in motion; what is in motion is not frozen; what is not frozen is liquid; what is liquid gives way. So logicians tell us that a dog, at a point where several paths meet, will argue from the exclusion of alternatives and will reason with himself as follows: the wild beast must have taken one of these three ways; it has certainly not taken this way and it has not taken this way; then it must have gone this way. Here perception gives nothing beyond the minor premiss; it is reason which supplies the major premisses and adds the conclusions. Not that the dog needs this kind of testimony, which happens to be false and spurious; for it is perception and nothing else – the perception of tracks or footprints – which shows the way the animal ran and for this disjunctive and copulative propositions are quite beside the point. But we can see what the dog is really like in very many other examples of how it acts and feels and performs

27. The Greek legend of the flood has Deucalion as its hero; but the detail about the dove, familiar from the story of Noah, seems to be an addition not found elsewhere in Greek sources.

its duties, cases where the senses of smell or sight do not enter in, but where action or perception can only be explained by the use of intelligence and reason. I should only be making a fool of myself if I were to tell you about the dog's self-control and obedience and quick apprehension when hunting. You see all this and have practical experience of it every day.

Let me turn to the case of Calvus,[28] a Roman who was killed in the Civil Wars. No one could cut off his head until they had formed a circle round him and stabbed to death his dog who was standing over his master and defending him. And once King Pyrrhus came across a dog on the road which was guarding the body of a man who had been murdered; he was told that the dog had stayed there for three days without food and would not leave the dead body. Pyrrhus ordered the corpse to be buried and told his men to take good care of the dog and bring it along with him. A few days later there was a review of the troops who marched past the king sitting on his throne; the dog was lying quietly by him until it saw the men who had murdered its master going past. Then it rushed out, barking furiously, and often turning its head round to the king as it was barking, so that not only he, but everyone else, became suspicious of the men. They were at once arrested and questioned; further evidence from outside was produced and the men confessed to the murder and were punished.

The poet Hesiod's dog is said to have done just the same thing in proving the guilt of Hesiod's murderers, the sons of Ganyctor of Naupactus. But an even clearer example than these was what happened in Athens and was known to our

28. The text of Plutarch is defective, and the name has been restored from Aelian, *De natura animalium*, 7. 10. There, however, some editors suppose that the emperor Galba is meant. The story of Pyrrhus that follows is also told by Aelian, loc. cit.

fathers when they were studying there.[29] A man made his way into the temple of Asclepius, stole all the gold and silver offerings that were easy to carry and got away again, thinking that no one had noticed him. But there was a watchdog called Capparus there who, when none of the priests paid any attention to his barking, went after the thief who was escaping with his haul of sacred objects. First of all the thief threw stones at him, but the dog kept on following. And when the sun rose, the dog still followed, not coming close, but never losing sight of him, and would not take the food the man offered him. When the man stopped to rest, the dog passed the night, still watching him; and when he started out again, the dog got up and followed. People he met on the road he would approach in a friendly way, but would keep barking at the thief and snapping at his heels. Those who were trying to trace the stolen goods heard of this from people who had met the dog and the man and they also described the colour and size of the dog. So they pressed the pursuit all the more vigorously, overtook the man, who had got as far as Crommyon and brought him back. The dog came with them, leading the procession, very pleased with himself and as happy as can be, as though he was asserting his claim to the full credit for tracing and arresting the robber of the temple. And in fact the people voted that the dog should be fed at the public expense and that the priests should be responsible for seeing to this as long as he lived. Here they were imitating the kindness shown by the Athenians of earlier times to the mule. This was when Pericles was building the Parthenon on the Acropolis. Every day, of course, great numbers of draught animals were used to bring up the stone, and of the mules there was one who had worked most nobly, but was

29. Presumably this dates the story to Plutarch's own youth; but it seems to be a common tale. (cf. Aelian, ibid., 7. 13, though this may be derived from Plutarch.)

discharged in the end because of old age. This mule used to go down every day to the Cerameicus and meet the other animals which were carrying up the stones. He would turn back with them and trot along at their side, as though urging them on and spurring them to greater effort. So the people of Athens, in admiration for its fine sense of honour and enterprise, ordered that it should be fed at the public's expense and voted it free meals, as for an athlete who had retired through old age.

14.[30] The view, therefore, that there are no relations involving justice between ourselves and animals must be admitted to be correct so far as animals which live in the water and the deep sea are concerned. These creatures are completely lacking in all amiable qualities; they know nothing of affection and there is nothing endearing in their characters. Homer very properly uses the words

> But the grey sea was your mother[31]

with reference to a man who appeared to be bitter and un-approachable, implying that the sea produces nothing kindly or gentle. But to use the same expressions of land animals would be in itself a mark of hard-heartedness and brutality. Was there no bond of justice and right feeling between Lysimachus and the Hyrcanian dog which stood as a solitary guard over his dead body and, when the body was cremated, rushed into the flames and threw itself upon him? And they say that the same thing was done by the eagle kept by Pyrrhus – not King Pyrrhus, but another man of the same name. When its master died it kept watch by the body and at the funeral it hovered just above the bier; and finally it folded its wings, settled on the pyre and was burned together with him.

And when King Porus[32] was wounded in the battle against

30. There is probably a passage missing before this chapter.
31. *Iliad*, 16. 34.   32. cf. Plutarch, *Alexander*, 60.

Alexander, his elephant carefully and gently pulled out with its trunk many of the javelins which were sticking in him. The elephant itself was in a bad way, but it did not give up until it realized that the king had lost a lot of blood and was slipping off; then, fearing that he might fall, it kneeled down very gently so that he could slide to the ground without hurting himself.

Bucephalus would let his groom mount him when he was unsaddled; but when he was decked out with all the royal trappings and neck ornaments he would not let anyone come near him except Alexander himself. If any of the others did try to approach, he would charge at them, neighing loudly, rearing up on his hind legs, and would trample them underfoot if they did not get out of the way first.

15. You will be thinking, I'm sure, that I'm choosing my examples in rather a random way; but with these noble creatures it's not at all easy to point to behaviour which will illustrate just one, and only one, of their virtues. In their care for their young there will be evidence also of their sense of honour; their docility will bear witness also to their generosity; and their cunning and intelligence is bound up with their high-spirited energy and their courage. However, if one wants to make fine distinctions and classifications one will find that dogs give the impression of being both civilized and high-minded when they turn away from and leave alone people who are sitting on the ground. No doubt this was what Homer referred to in the lines:

Barking the dogs rushed out to attack him there, but Odysseus
Cleverly crouched to the ground and let the staff fall from his hands.[33]

For dogs will leave one alone if one sinks down to the ground and takes up a humble and conciliatory attitude.

We are told too of the dog who was leader of the pack of

33. *Odyssey*, 14. 30 f.

Alexander's Indian hunting-dogs and was much admired by Alexander himself. When first a stag, then a wild boar and then a bear was let loose in front of him, this dog just lay still and showed no interest; but when a lion came in sight, it sprang up at once and made ready for battle, obviously showing that, while it despised the rest, it had found in the lion a worthy antagonist.

And you will find that with dogs that hunt hares, so long as they have killed the animal themselves, they will enjoy tearing its flesh and will eagerly lap up the blood. But if, as often happens, the hare in a last desperate burst of speed uses up all the breath in its body and drops down dead, the dogs, when they find the corpse, do not even touch it; they stand there wagging their tails, as if to say that what they have been straining for is not flesh to eat, but victory and the honour that goes with it.

16. Many examples of cunning in animals can be given. But here I shall leave aside foxes and wolves and the clever tricks of cranes and jackdaws, since these are perfectly well known. The witness I shall bring forward is Thales, the most ancient of the Wise Men, one of whose most remarkable achievements, they say, was the trick by which he got the better of a mule. One of the mules used for carrying salt happened to fall down when it was fording a river. The salt melted away and when it got up, the heavy load was gone. The mule realized what the cause was and kept it in mind with the result that every time it crossed the river it would deliberately sink down into the water and get the bags wet, sitting right down and rolling first to one side, then to the other. When Thales heard of this he told the muleteers to put wool and sponges instead of salt inside the bags, and make the mule carry these. The mule behaved as usual and soaked its load in the water, but then discovered that the trick had not turned out at all well for it. And in future it was so careful and

cautious in crossing the river that not even by accident did the water touch the load it was carrying.

Partridges have a clever trick which is associated with their love for their young. They teach the fledglings, who are still unable to fly, to lie on their backs when pursued and to hold out above them as a screen a tuft of grass or scrap of rubbish. Meanwhile the mother birds draw off the hunters in another direction and attract attention to themselves by fluttering along just in front of them, only rising a little from the ground and making it look as though they are on the point of being captured. This goes on until they have led the hunters far away from the young birds.

When hares go to rest for the night, they put their leverets to sleep in different places, often as much as a hundred feet apart, so that if a man or a dog comes on the scene they will not all be in danger at once. And the hares themselves run about here and there, leaving tracks in many directions, and then finally with a great long leap they spring clear of their tracks and go to bed.

The she-bear, just before the period called hibernation, and when she is still not quite torpid and sluggish and slow on her feet, cleans out her lair and, when just about to go down into it, she comes up to it on tip-toe, treading as lightly and carefully as she can, and then backs into it and lowers herself down into her winter quarters.

Hinds may often give birth to their young close to a highway where carnivorous animals do not come. And stags, when they realize that fat and surplus flesh has made them put on too much weight, go off into hiding and preserve themselves in this way, no longer being able to rely on their speed of foot.

The hedgehog's method of self-defence has given rise to the proverb:

The fox knows many things, the hedgehog one great thing.[34]

34. Attributed to Archilochus and to Homer.

For when the fox appears, the hedgehog, as Ion[35] says:

> Will curl its prickly body up into a ball,
> Hopeless to touch or bite, and lie there low.

But there is something even more subtle about the way they plan ahead for their young. In the autumn the hedgehog creeps under the vines and uses its paws to shake the grapes down to the ground from the branches. It then rolls about on them and gets up with them sticking to its spines. I saw one when I was a child and it looked like a creeping or walking bunch of grapes. Then it goes down into its lair and lets the young unload the grapes from it and keep them for future distribution. The hedgehog's lair has two openings, one facing north and one south; and when they realize that the wind is going to change, they block up the windward entrance and open up the other one, just like sea-captains shifting sail. There was, indeed, a man in Cyzicus who had noticed this and who got a great reputation for being able to predict entirely by himself which way the wind would blow.

17. Elephants, as Juba[36] tells us, show not only intelligence but feeling for the community. Hunters dig pits for them, covering them over with twigs and brushwood. Now when one elephant out of a herd all travelling together falls in, the others bring wood and stones and throw them in to fill up the hole so that the trapped animal can get out easily. Juba also tells us that, without any instruction, they pray to the gods, purifying themselves in the sea, and adoring the sun when it rises by stretching out their trunks like hands spread out in worship. They are therefore dearer to the gods than any other animal. This is shown by the case of Ptolemy

35. Fr. 38.

36. 275 F 51 in F. Jacoby, *Fragmente der Griechisches Historiker*, III A, Leiden, 1940. Juba II of Numidia was brought to Rome by Caesar and educated there.

Philopator,[37] who after his victory over Antiochus wanted to show particular honour to the gods and among many other offerings of thanks for the victory sacrificed four elephants. After that his sleep was troubled by dreams showing that heaven was angry with him and was threatening him because of such a monstrous sacrifice. So he carried out a number of ceremonies to soothe the anger of the gods and dedicated four bronze elephants to make up for those he had slaughtered.

There is an equal feeling for the community among lions. The young lions take the old and slow-footed ones along with them when they go hunting; and when the old ones get tired, they sit down and wait while the young ones go on with the hunt. And when these have made their kill, they call the others, roaring in a way very like the bleating of a calf. The old lions hear it at once and come up to take their share in what has been caught.

18. Some animals behave in a very savage and frenzied way when they are in love; but others show a delicacy which is quite human and a real charm in their sexual relations. For example, there was the elephant at Alexandria who was the rival of Aristophanes, the grammarian. They were both in love with the same flower-girl and the elephant was not at all behindhand in showing it. He always brought fruit for her whenever he passed by the market and would stand at her side for a long time and would put his trunk, as though it were a hand, inside her dress and gently stroke her lovely breasts.

The snake that fell in love with an Aetolian woman used to visit her at night, slip in under her body next to the skin and twine itself round her. It never hurt her in any way either intentionally or accidentally and went away very politely at daybreak. And it continued to behave like this until the woman's relations moved her into another house some way

37. Defeated Antiochus at Raphia in 217.

off. For three or four nights after that the snake did not come to her. Most probably it was wandering about looking for her. And in the end after some difficulty it did find her, but then instead of embracing her in its usual gentle way, it was rather rough; coiling round her, it pinioned her arms to her sides and lashed the calves of her legs with the end of its tail in a kind of anger that was still affectionate and not very serious and more inclined to spare her pain than to inflict it.

Then there are the famous stories of the goose in Aegium that loved a boy and the ram that fell in love with Glauce, the harp-player.[38] But I expect you've heard these told so often that you are sick of them, so I won't mention them here.

19. I regard starlings and crows and parrots which learn to talk as the leading advocates for all other animals in so far as capacity for learning is concerned. These birds can produce for their teachers a most wonderful voice control and power of mimicry all ready to be trained exactly, and the lesson which they somehow impart to us is that they too can articulate and speak intelligently. And so it seems utterly absurd to bring them into comparison with creatures whose vocal powers do not extend so far as a howl or a groan. As for the delightful music in natural, untaught bird-song, our own best and most melodious poets bear witness to that when they compare their sweetest songs and poems to the singing of swans and nightingales. And since teaching requires more of the reasoning faculty than learning, we must now take Aristotle's word for it that animals do teach; a nightingale, he says, has been observed teaching her young to sing. Evidence that supports him here is in the fact that birds which have been taken young from the nest and separated from their mothers do not sing so well as the others. Birds brought up with their mothers are taught by them and they do not learn

38. These stories also in Aelian, *De natura animalium*, 5. 29, 12. 37, etc.

to sing because of any reward or reputation, but for the sheer pleasure of musical competition and the delight in the beauty rather than in the utility of their song.

On this subject I can tell you a story which I heard from many Greeks and Romans who were actually there at the time. There was a barber in Rome who had his shop just opposite the quarter known as the Greek market. This barber had an absolutely wonderful jay. It could use its voice in all kinds of ways, imitating human speech, the cries of birds and animals and the sound of instruments. And no one tried to force the bird to do this; the bird was its own trainer; it felt that its honour was involved in being able to pronounce and to imitate everything it heard. But it happened that there was a funeral, accompanied by many trumpets, of a rich man from the district and, as was usual, the procession halted outside the barber's shop and there the trumpeters went on playing for a long time, since everyone was applauding them and telling them to go on. From that day the jay was speechless and dumb. Not even when it wanted something urgently would it make a sound. Habitual passers-by, who used to wonder at the bird's voice, were now equally astonished by the blank and total silence. It was suspected that the jay had been poisoned by rival bird-fanciers, but the general opinion was that it had been deafened by the noise of the trumpets and that it had lost the power of speech together with its power of hearing. Both conjectures, however, were wrong. It was rather, it seems, a case of self-discipline; the mimetic powers had gone into a retreat of introspection while the bird was tuning up her voice and preparing it like a musical instrument. Suddenly it came back and blazed out again in full glory. And this time, instead of the well-known imitations of the past, what came out was the music of the trumpets, with the intervals exactly kept, and every change of pitch and rhythm followed precisely. And so, as I said before, this power of self-instruction which we find in animals requires more of the reasoning faculty than the power to learn from others.

But I think I must give you just one example of a dog's ability to learn. I saw this myself in a theatre in Rome. This dog was appearing in a pantomime which had a connected plot and a number of different characters. It acted very well, doing just the things and showing just the feelings required by the text. And in particular they tried a drug on him which was really soporific, but which, according to the plot, was supposed to be poison. The dog took the bread that was supposed to be poisoned, swallowed it and a little later seemed to shiver and go weak at the knees and heavy in the head. Finally it fell to the ground and lay there stretched out like a corpse, just as according to the stage direction. But when it recognized from the dialogue and the action that the moment had come, it began at first to stir slightly, as though it was coming to from a heavy sleep, and lifted its head up and looked around. Then to everyone's amazement, it got to its feet and went straight to the right person, wagging its tail with joy and affection. Everyone was deeply moved, even Caesar himself; for Vespasian in his old age was there, in the Theatre of Marcellus.

20. But perhaps it is rather ridiculous of us to make so much of animals' ability to learn, when Democritus tells us[39] that in the most important things it is we who have learned from the animals. We learned from the spider how to weave, from the swallow how to build houses, and by imitating the singing birds, the swan and the nightingale, we learned how to sing ourselves. Then we see that animals are endowed, and richly endowed, with knowledge of each of the three[40] branches of medicine. It is not only drugs of which they make use,

39. Democritus, fr. 154 in M. Diels and W. Kranz (eds.), *Die Fragmente der Vorsokratiker*, 6th ed., Berdin, 1954.
40. These, as appears later, are cures by drugs, by diet and by surgery.

though there are plenty of examples of the use of drugs. After eating a snake, tortoises, for instance, will eat marjoram and weasels will eat rue. Dogs, when in a bilious condition, purge themselves by eating grass. Snakes with failing eyesight use fennel to give them a sharper and clearer vision. When the she-bear comes out from her winter lair, the first thing she eats is wild arum; the bitterness of this plant has an aperient effect on her bowels which have become constipated. And if at any time she suffers from nausea, she looks for ant-hills and sits in front of them holding out her tongue, which is all coated and dripping with a sweet-tasting kind of exudation. Soon her tongue is covered with ants and she swallows these and feels much better. The Egyptians say that they have observed how the ibis uses salt-water, as it were an enema, to purge itself and that they have imitated the bird in this. And they use water from which the ibis has drunk to purify themselves. This is because the ibis will never go near any water that is not perfectly fresh and wholesome.

Some animals also will take care of their health by abstaining from food. Among these are wolves and lions, who, when they have had enough flesh to eat, lie quietly down and bask in the sun. And they say that if one gives a kid to a tigress, she will start dieting and eat nothing for two days; on the third she gets hungry and demands some other food; she will even tear her cage to pieces, but will not touch the kid whom she now regards as a friend and room-mate.

Surgery too, we are informed, is practised by elephants. They will come to the help of the wounded and skilfully draw out spears and javelins and arrows without causing pain or tearing the flesh. And the goats in Crete by eating dittany can easily get rid of arrows sticking in their bodies. They have thus made it quite easy for pregnant women to discover that this plant has an abortive property, since dittany is the one thing that goats rush off to look for when they are wounded.

21. All this is wonderful enough; but still more wonderful are those creatures, like the cattle near Susa, which have the concept of number and the ability to count. At Susa the king's park is irrigated by water drawn up in buckets by wheels. The number of bucketsful is fixed at one hundred a day for each cow, and you would not get a cow to raise more than one hundred even if you wanted to use force. In fact they often try the experiment of adding to the load; but the cow backs away and won't have any of it; she has delivered the quota. For this extraordinary accuracy in counting and in remembering the sum my evidence is Ctesias of Cnidus.[41]

The Egyptian story about the oryx is regarded by the Libyans as a ridiculous fabrication. But according to the Egyptians the oryx raises a cry on the day and at the precise hour of the rising of the star which they call Sothis and we call the Dog Star or Sirius. And at any rate, they say, nearly all the goats turn round and look towards the east just when the star rises in a direct line with the sun; and they regard this as the most certain indication of its periodic return, agreeing precisely with their mathematical tables.

22. But now let me bring my speech to its final climax and reach the height of my argument by saying a few words about the divine inspiration and prophetic powers of animals. You will agree that what is called bird-lore, far from being a small or unworthy branch of prophecy, is extremely ancient and very important. Birds, with their quickness of apprehension and their ability to change direction in response to any suggestion, are like an instrument ready to the hand of the divine power who uses and controls their movements, their calls or cries, and their flight formation, making them just like winds, sometimes unfavourable and sometimes favourable, checking some actions and projects, and directing others

41. Greek physician at the Persian court, fourth century B.C.; historian.

to their fulfilment. It is because of this that Euripides calls birds in general 'heralds of the gods';[42] and Socrates,[43] in particular, says that he claims to be 'fellow-slave of the swans'. Or to take kings; Pyrrhus liked to be called an eagle and Antiochus a hawk. But when we are mocking or abusing some ignorant blockhead what we call him is 'a poor fish'. In fact one could produce hundreds of thousands of examples of signs and prophecies revealed to us by the gods through birds and land animals, whereas not a single one could be brought forward by the spokesman for aquatic creatures. In fact these creatures are all 'deaf and blind' so far as any foresight is concerned and have been cast out into an area reserved for the godless and the primitive – a sort of hell, where what is rational and intelligent in the soul has been extinguished. What little sensation they have left is buried in the mud or drowned in water and what life they have is more like a convulsive struggle for air.

23. HERACLEON: Phaedimus, my friend, we, the islanders and the people by the sea, now turn to you. Look as fierce as you can and rouse yourself for battle. This argument has turned out to be no laughing matter. You have a very stiff case on your hands and it has been presented with such force that one could imagine oneself actually in a court of law.

PHAEDIMUS: Not at all, Heracleon. What we have to deal with is, quite obviously, a cleverly laid ambush. Here we are, still a bit fuddled and under the weather from yesterday's drinking, and my distinguished friend who is, as you see, stone-cold sober, has carefully chosen this moment to attack us. But there can be no crying-off. I am a great admirer of Pindar, but I don't want to have these words of his quoted at me:

> To make excuses once the lists are open
> Envelops valour in an utter darkness.[44]

42. Perhaps *Ion*, 159.   43. Plato, *Phaedo*, 85 B.   44. Fr. 228.

We have plenty of time on our hands. Today because of our argument a truce has been granted to every creature on land and sea. So while our dogs and horses and hunting and fishing nets are out of employment, our tongues will be active. But don't be alarmed. I shall use my time with discretion and shall avoid bringing in theories of philosophers, fairy stories from Egypt or unattested stories of Indians or Libyans. I shall just put before you a few examples of fact that can be observed everywhere, which can be vouched for by men who make the sea their occupation and whose credibility is that of eye witnesses.

I should point out, however, that in the case of land animals there is no difficulty in finding one's examples; the land is wide open for the senses to gather information from it. The sea, on the other hand, only allows a limited and imperfect vision of what goes on. The birth and growth, the methods of attack and self-defence are for most of her creatures lost to sight. And so our argument must suffer because many actions showing intelligence, memory and feeling for the community are simply not known to us. Then too, land animals because of their close relationship and shared way of life with men have to some extent been affected by human manners; they have the advantage of being bred and trained by men and being able to imitate them; and this, like fresh water mixed with salt, has a sweetening effect on all their bitterness and sullenness; all their stupidity and slowness are stirred into activity by their contact with human beings. But the life of sea creatures is utterly set apart and divided from the society of man; there have been no importations, nothing learnt from others; it is a thing to itself, indigenous and uncontaminated by outside influence. And this is not because of Nature, but is simply a question of geography. So far as Nature is concerned, sea creatures will welcome and retain any learning that comes their way. This accounts for the docility of many eels, such as those which are called sacred in Arethusa. And there are many examples of fish that will answer to their own names. For instance, the lamprey owned by Crassus. The story is that when this lamprey died, Crassus burst into tears; and once Domitius said to him 'Is it true that you burst into tears when a lamprey died?' To which Crassus answered, 'And is it true that you buried three wives without shedding a tear at all?'

The crocodiles kept by the priests not only recognize the priests' voices when they call them and allow themselves to be handled, but open their jaws to have their teeth cleaned and then wiped with towels. And our good friend Philinus, back from his travels in Egypt, told us that in Antaeopolis he saw an old woman sleeping on the same low bed with a crocodile. The crocodile was stretched out beside her and behaving admirably in every way.

There is also a very old story about King Ptolemy who, they say, called the sacred crocodile, but it would not listen to him or do as it was told. The priests took this to be an omen that the King would die as indeed he did soon afterwards. So far then as your celebrated power of prophecy is concerned, it would appear that aquatic creatures have it too and are well known for it. In fact I hear that near Sura, which is a village in Lycia between Phellus and Myra, people sit and watch the fish turning and twisting in pursuit or escape and can predict the future from their movements, as others do with birds, in accordance with a rational system.

24. I think I have said enough to show that these aquatic animals are not entirely alien and unrelated to us. As for their own particular and innate intelligence, this is very clearly shown by their quick reaction to danger. Excluding those creatures that fasten on the rocks and stick there, there is no swimming creature that can easily be got hold of by man or caught without a lot of trouble, as asses are by wolves, bees

by bee-eaters, cicadas by swallows and snakes by deer. Deer easily attract snakes and the proper derivation of their name, *elaphoi*, is not from *elaphros* (light-footed) but from *hel-* = (attract) and *ophis* (a snake).[45] So too the ram attracts the wolf by stamping on the ground and they say that many animals are attracted towards their enemies because they enjoy the smell of them; apes, in particular, are attracted in this way by panthers. But in practically all sea-creatures sensation leads immediately to suspicion and to an intelligent anticipation of impending attack. The result is that there is nothing simple or casual about fishing; in dealing with fish one needs all kinds of equipment and all sorts of tricks and stratagems.

There are plenty of examples ready to hand. One's rod must not be too thick, though it must be pliable so as to stand up to the thrashing about of a fish when it is on the hook; what one chooses is a slender rod, so that it will not cast a broad shadow which would arouse the fish's suspicion. Then one will avoid having a number of knots in the line or thickening it, since this too will be taken by the fish as a sign of something wrong. And one will see that in one's line the hairs nearest to the hook are as white as possible so that, being of much the same colour as the sea, they will not be easily noticed. The lines of the poet:[46]

Then to the depths of the sea she sank down deep like the lead weight
Fixed inside the horn of the country-wandering ox.
And bringing down to the greedy fish their doom and destruction

are misunderstood by some people who take them to mean that in old times ox-hair was used for fishing lines; for they claim that *keras* (horn) means hair and that this accounts for the words *keirasthai* (to have one's hair cut) and *koura* (a lock

45. An absurd derivation.
46. Homer, *Iliad*, 24. 80–82.

of hair); and the word *keroplastes*[47] in Archilochus[48] means a person who pays particular attention to having his hair well cut and dressed. But this is not the case. What is used is horse-hair taken from the male horse, because the mares get the hair wet from their urine and so weaken it. And Aristarchus says that there is nothing out-of-the-way or obscure in these lines; the reference is to the small tube of horn which surrounds the line just above the hook; without this horn tube the fish would bite through the line. As for the hooks themselves, rounded ones are used to catch mullets and bonitos, which have small mouths and which are scared by a broad hook. In fact a mullet is often suspicious even of a rounded hook and swims all round it, flipping the bait with its tail and gobbling up the bits that it shakes loose, or if it can't do this, it purses up its mouth and nibbles at the bait with just the tips of its lips.

The sea-bass is braver than the elephant. With him it is not a question of dragging weapons out of another's body; he will perform the operation on himself when he is caught on the hook; then he will shake his head from side to side, widening the wound and enduring the pain from the tearing of his flesh, until he can get rid of the hook. The fox-shark is very wary of any bait and very seldom comes near the hook. However, if he is caught, he will immediately turn himself inside out; nature has provided him with a kind of tension and pliability which enables him to twist and wriggle his body into such a posture that, with the inside outside, the hook simply falls out.

25. These creatures make it clear that fish have intelligence and that, when the time comes, they use it in a remarkably clever way for their own advantage. But I can give you other

47. Really refers to a style of hair-dressing in curls like horns.

48. Fr. 59, in E. Diehl (ed.), *Anthologia Lyrica Graeca*, 3rd ed. Leipzig, 1949–52.

examples which will show not only intelligence but a sense for the community and an altruistic affection. Let us take the barbier and the parrot fish. If a parrot fish swallows the hook, all the others who are around will swarm up towards the line and nibble through it. And when some of them have been caught in a net, the others will come up and from outside will give them their tails; the fish in the net will bite hard on the tails and will then be dragged out in tow by the others. And barbiers make even greater exertions to help their fellow barbiers. They will set their backs under the line, raise their sharp spines and try to saw it and cut it through with the rough edge of their barbs.

Yet we know of no land animal – no bear, or boar, or lioness or panther – which has the courage to come to the help of another in danger. You may say that in the arena animals of the same species will draw together and huddle into a circle. But they neither know how to help each other nor are even thinking of it. What each of them is doing is simply to run away and get as far as possible from a wounded or dying fellow. And as for that story of yours about elephants carrying brush-wood to the pits and making a ramp to rescue those who have fallen in, that is really fantastically far-fetched. Or are we meant to believe it as it were on royal command, simply because it comes from the writings of Juba? Even if it were true, all it would prove is that in intelligence and feeling for the community there are a great many sea creatures who are not in the least inferior to the wisest of all the land animals. But I shall have something particular to say presently about the subject of their community feeling.

26. Fishermen have come to realize that most fish can evade the strike of a hook as skilfully as wrestlers slip out of a hold. They have therefore, like the Persians,[49] resorted to brute force and taken to the use of the drag-net on the assumption that

49. Herodotus, *History*, 6, 31.

for those caught in it no intelligence or cleverness would provide an escape. Thus there are casting-nets and round nets used for catching mullet, rainbow-wrasse, bream, sargue, goby and sea-bass. What are known as net-fish, such as the surmullet, gilthead and sculpin are caught in seines by trawling. So Homer is quite correct in calling this kind of net 'all-catching'.[50] But cod have ways of dealing with this too, as have bass. When the bass realizes that the trawl is coming near, it scrapes and shovels a hollow in the sea bottom and when it has cleared enough space to allow the net to go by overhead, it burrows inside and stays there till the net has gone past.

When the dolphin is caught and realizes that it is trapped in the net, it just stays where it is; far from being upset, it is delighted, since without any trouble to itself it can have a regular feast on all the fish that are there; but as soon as the net gets near the shore, the dolphin bites through it and is away. And if it fails to get away in time, nothing serious happens to it on the first occasion: the fishermen merely sew rushes to its dorsal fin near the head and let it go. But if it is caught again they recognize it from the rushes attached to it and beat it as a punishment. This, however, hardly ever happens. Most dolphins who have been forgiven once are grateful for it and take care not to do any harm in future.

I could give you plenty more examples to show how these creatures can foresee, guard against or evade danger. And among these I must certainly not forget to mention the cuttle-fish. This creature has at the side of its neck the organ known as the mytis, which is full of a black liquid which they call ink. When it is surprised, it discharges this liquid; then, with the sea all inked out, it folds itself in darkness and achieves its purpose of escaping and slipping away out of the fisherman's

50. *Iliad*, 5. 486.

sight, just like the gods in Homer who often 'in a dark cloud'[51] snatch up and carry away those whose lives they want to save. Enough, however, of this.

27. Let me now turn to the cleverness they show in attacking and catching their prey. Their skill here can be observed in many different species. The star-fish, for instance, is well aware that everything to which it attaches itself will dissolve and go liquid; and so it presents its body to other creatures which come up to it or pass it by and allows them to come in contact with it. You know, of course, about the electric ray and what it can do; it not only paralyses those who touch it but even through the net produces a heavy narcotic feeling in the hands of the trawlers. And according to some who have experimented further with it, if it is washed ashore alive and you pour water on it from above, you will feel a numbness coming up into your hands and dulling the sense of touch; this, presumably, is conducted to you by way of the water which has already been affected and altered in quality. The fish itself has an innate sense of this power and so it never attacks anything directly or endangers itself; instead it swims in a circle around its prey and lets loose its shocks like darts; the poison affects the water first and then, through the water, the creature itself which can neither defend itself nor escape; it is chained fast where it is and frozen stiff.

The frog called the fisherman is well known and gets his name from what he does. And Aristotle says that the cuttle-fish also makes use of this trick: he lets down from his neck, like a fishing line, a tentacle which is naturally designed to extend longer and longer when released and to fold back again when drawn in. So when he sees one of the little fishes coming near, he gives it the tentacle to bite and then gradually and imperceptibly draws it in until it is held fast and in reach of his mouth.

51. e.g. *Iliad*, 5. 345.

As for the change of colour in the octopus, Pindar[52] has celebrated it in the words:

> Bring to all the cities where you stay
> A mind most like the skin of the sea beast.

And Theognis[53] too:

> Take to yourself the mind of the octopus changing in colour:
> As is the rock where he clings, so is his colour to see.

The chameleon, of course, also changes colour; but he does not do this with any end in view or to hide himself. He is naturally cowardly and terrified at the slightest sound and he changes colour quite pointlessly out of terror. This, according to Theophrastus, is the natural result of the quantity of air inside; nearly the whole of this creature's body is occupied by its lungs, which shows that it is full of air and, for this reason, liable to change colour easily. But when the octopus changes colour it is a positive action, not a mere reflex. The change is made deliberately as a device for escaping from creatures it is afraid of and for getting hold of those on which it lives; by this mode of deception it is able to seize the latter who do not try to escape, and to evade the former, who simply pass it by. The story that it eats its own tentacles is quite untrue; but it is true that it is afraid of the lamprey and the conger. It suffers a lot from them and is unable to do anything about it since they can slip out of its grasp. On the other hand the crawfish can deal with them easily once he has a grip on them; their smooth skins are no help against his jagged pincers. Yet if the octopus once gets its tentacles inside a crawfish, the crawfish is finished. By this cycle and system of pursuit and flight, flight and pursuit, Nature has set up for these creatures a discipline and a kind of training ground for competitive exercise in skill and intelligence.

52. Fr. 43.   53. 215–16.

28. You will remember that Aristotimus told us about the hedgehog's ability to forecast the direction of the wind; and he also admired the wedge formation of cranes in flight. Personally I can't produce any single hedgehogs from Cyzicus or Byzantium, but I can point to the entire population of sea-urchins. These, when they realize that stormy weather and rough seas are on the way, ballast themselves with little stones, so that they may stay fixed where they are by the weight of their bits of stone and not be knocked off their balance or swept away because they are too light when the storm comes.

As for the way the cranes change direction so as to fly into the wind, this is not a peculiarity of any one species; generally speaking, all fish have the same idea and always swim against the direction of the waves and current; they are careful to see that pressure from the rear does not fold back their scales and expose and roughen their bodies. So they always meet the waves head-on, since in this way the sea-water cleft by their heads, presses down their gills, flows smoothly over the surface of their bodies and smooths down, rather than ruffles up, their fins. This, as I said, is the way all fish behave. The exception is the sturgeon who, they say, swims with the wind and tide and is not afraid of having his scales ruffled up, the reason being that the overlaps are not in the direction of the tail.

29. The tunny has such a keen perception of equinox and solstice that, without any astronomical tables, he can provide men themselves with accurate information of when they come. Wherever it may be at the time of the winter solstice, it stays in or around that place until the coming of the equinox.

And as for that clever trick of the crane gripping a stone during the night so as to be woken up if it slips out of its grasp – how much cleverer, my friend, is what the dolphin does. With the dolphin it is a law never to stay still, never to rest from motion; its nature is to be always moving and immobility to it spells death. When it is in need of sleep, it rises up to the surface of the sea and then, lying on its back, lets itself sink down into the depths, rocked to sleep by the sway of the swell, until it touches the bottom. Then it wakes up and comes dashing up to the surface where it again lets itself relax and sinks down. And so it has thought out for itself a method of combining rest with motion. And they say that tunnies do the same thing for the same reason.

A few moments ago I was telling you of the tunny's mathematical foreknowledge of the sun's change of course (a fact to which Aristotle testifies). Now I'd like to tell you about their knowledge of arithmetic. But first I really must mention their knowledge of optics. This is something which it seems Aeschylus knew of, as he writes somewhere:

And squinting like a tunny-fish with his left eye.[54]

They do, in fact, appear to have bad sight in one eye. And this is why, when they enter the Black Sea, they keep close to the shore on the right and keep to the opposite shore when they are on their way out – a most intelligent and sensible procedure which ensures that they always have the use of the better eye for self-protection.

As for arithmetic, it seems that they need this because of their community spirit and the affection which they feel for each other, and they have brought their knowledge to such a high standard that, since they take particular pleasure in feeding all together in a school, they invariably form the school into a cube, a perfectly solid figure of six equal plane sides. They then swim on their way, keeping this formation in a square facing both ways. Certainly the man on watch for tunnies, once he makes a correct estimate of the number on

54. Fr. 308.

the surface, can tell you at once how many there are in the entire shoal, since he knows that the depth is exactly equal to the breadth and to the length.

30. The habit of going about in schools has given the bonitos their name of *amia*,[55] a word that is also used, I think, of year-old tunnies. As for all the other kinds of fish which are observed to live a community life together in shoals, they are far too many to mention. Let me turn instead to those which live together in the special relationship of symbiosis. One of these is the pinna-guard, and Chrysippus has used up a vast quantity of ink in writing about it; in fact in every one of his books, whether on ethics or natural history, it has a place of honour. Apparently Chrysippus has not studied the sponge-guard; otherwise he would certainly have mentioned it too. The pinna-guard is, so they say, a crab-like creature which lives with the pinna and sits in front of the shell guarding the entrance. It allows the pinna to keep its shell wide open until one of the little fish on which it feeds gets inside. Then the guard nips the flesh of the pinna and slips inside the shell; the shell shuts and the two of them together feed on the prey which is enclosed.

The little creature that takes charge of the sponge looks more like a spider than a crab. And the sponge, though like many other creatures it clings to the rocks, is not a lifeless, insensitive, bloodless thing. It has the power to move on its own by contraction and expansion, but this movement requires stimulus and supervision. It is loose in texture and because of its dull and lazy nature, the pores tend to be relaxed. But when anything edible comes into its embrace, the guard gives the signal, and it closes up and devours what it has caught. And, even more remarkable, when a man comes near or touches it, it is made aware of this by the scratching of the guard and it gives a kind of shudder and folds in on

55. Supposedly meaning 'not alone' and probably a false derivation.

itself by stiffening and contracting so that it is far from easy – in fact it is very difficult – for the sponge fishers to cut it loose.

The purple-fish lives in colonies and the whole colony joins together in building a comb, like bees, in which they are said to breed. And by means of the edible bits of oyster-grass and seaweed that get attached to the shells they provide themselves with a sort of banquet that goes on all the year round, as each takes his turn in feeding another.

31. Nor is there any reason to be surprised at the fellow-feeling shown by these creatures when one considers that the crocodile, the most anti-social and brutal of all animals bred in rivers, lakes or sea, shows himself in his relations with the Egyptian plover extraordinarily well adapted to a shared way of life with mutual goodwill. The plover is a bird of the marshes and river banks; it guards the crocodile and, instead of supplying its own food, is fed, like a lodger, on scraps that the crocodile has left over. When the plover becomes aware that the ichneumon, smearing itself with mud like an athlete rubbing dust on his limbs, is planning an attack on the crocodile while it is asleep, it wakes the crocodile up by pecking at it and uttering cries. And the crocodile is so gentle with the plover that it will open its mouth and let the bird inside and be delighted while it quietly pecks out with its bill bits of meat which have got caught in the teeth, cleaning them in the process. When the crocodile has had enough of this and wants to close its mouth, it gives the signal by tilting its snout upwards and does not close its jaws until the plover has taken the hint and flown out.

The fish known as 'the leader' is a small fish like a goby in size and shape, but, so they say, the roughness of its scales make it look more like a bird with ruffled feathers. It always goes in company with one of the big whales and swims in front, guiding it on its course so that it will not run aground in shallow water or get itself into some lagoon or restricted space from which it might be difficult to get out. The whale follows it, as a ship obeys the rudder, and changes course as directed. And whatever else is taken in by the whale's great jaws, whether living creature or boat or rock, is at once lost and entirely engulfed; but the whale knows this little fish and will take it inside his mouth as safely as into a harbour. While the fish sleeps inside, the whale stays where he is and lies by; but when the fish comes out again, the whale follows it and keeps with it day and night; otherwise it will get lost and wander aimlessly or, as often happens, be thrown up on land and die there, like ships without a pilot. As a matter of fact we saw an example of this not long ago near Anticyra; and they say that quite recently when a whale got washed ashore not far from Bouna and rotted, it caused a plague.

To my mind these examples of fellow-feeling and companionship are more reputable than are the friendships which Aristotle tells us exist between foxes and snakes because of their common hostility to the eagle, or between bustards and horses because the birds enjoy the proximity and the picking over of dung. In fact even in ants or bees I fail to see that there is any such concern for one another. Certainly they do all join together in furthering the common interest; but they show not the faintest thought for or interest in each other as individuals.

32. And we shall see the difference even more clearly when we turn to the subject of birth and procreation, a subject with which the oldest established and the most important of social actions and obligations are concerned. In the first place, fish that live in a sea that opens into lagoons or receives the influx of rivers go to the rivers and lagoons when they are ready to deposit their eggs. What they look for is the mildness and the freshness of water that is not salt, since perfect calm is the right environment for birth. Then too enclosed waters and rivers are free from large sea creatures and this gives the young fish

a better chance of survival. This is why so many fish are particularly fond of the Black Sea for spawning; it has no large sea creatures at all apart from an occasional seal or a small dolphin; also the influx of river water – and a number of very big rivers flow into the Black Sea – produces a mild blend of water that is very good for breeding.

There is a most extraordinary thing about the *anthias*, which Homer[56] calls the sacred fish. Though many people think that the word 'sacred' just means important, as we call the last bone in the spine *os sacrum* because it is important, and epilepsy the 'sacred disease' for the same reason. Others take it in the usual sense of dedicated or consecrated. Eratosthenes, it seems, is referring to the gilt-head when he writes:

Swift on the course, with gold on his brow, the fish that is sacred.[56a]

Though many say that it is the sturgeon, which is rare and difficult to catch. It is often to be seen, however, off the coast of Pamphylia and when fishermen do manage to catch one, they put garlands on their heads and wreathe them around their boats and, as they sail past, they are greeted and honoured with shouting and loud applause. Most people, however, think that the sacred fish is the *anthias* and that it is to him that the adjective refers. For wherever the *anthias* is seen there are no predatory fish. Sponge fishers can dive and fish can spawn in perfect confidence as though their security was guaranteed. The reason for this is obscure. It may be that predators avoid the *anthias* as elephants avoid a pig or lions a cock; or it may be that there are some things which indicate the absence of dangerous creatures and that the *anthias*, being

56. Homer speaks of 'sacred fish', *Iliad*, 6. 407. He does not mention the *anthias*.

56a. Eratosthenes, Fr. 12, in J. U. Powell, *Collectanea Alexandrina*, Oxford, 1925.

an intelligent fish and gifted with memory, comes to know these indications and stays around where they are.

33. Forethought and care for the young is common to both parents. The males do not eat their own young; they stay by the spawn, as Aristotle tells us, and keep guard over the eggs. Some follow behind the female and sprinkle their sperm gradually over the eggs; otherwise the spawn will not grow properly, but will remain defective and undeveloped. And the wrasse will go off on his own and construct a kind of nest out of seaweed and envelop the spawn in it to protect it from the waves.

And as regards affection for their young, not the tamest and most domestic animal shows more warmth and gentleness than the dog-fish. First the egg is laid and then they nurse and carry along the newly-hatched fish, not outside but actually inside their own bodies, as though it had been born twice over. When the young grow bigger, the parents let them out and teach them to swim close by; and then they take them in again through their mouths and let them use their bodies as a home where they can find room and food and security until they are strong enough to look after themselves.

It is wonderful too what care the turtle takes over the birth and preservation of her young. She comes a short distance out of the sea to lay her eggs; but since she is unable to incubate them or to stay long on dry land, she deposits them in a hole on the beach and covers them over with the smoothest and softest sand she can find. After she has buried them and hidden them safely, according to some accounts she scratches over the ground with her feet, leaving marks which she will easily be able to recognize; though others say that the peculiar marks and impressions which she leaves behind are because she has been turned over on her back by the male. But more wonderful still is the fact that she waits for forty days, which is the time required by the eggs to develop, and hatch out, and then comes back again. Each turtle knows just where her own treasure is buried and opens it up with all the joy and the eagerness that a man would show over a hidden store of gold.

34. The crocodile behaves in much the same way, except that here no one has been able to guess or to produce any rational explanation of how it is that the animal knows exactly the right place to go and for this reason it is supposed that the crocodile's knowledge comes from divine inspiration rather than reason. She comes out of the water to lay her eggs to precisely the distance, no more and no less, which will be covered that season by the Nile in flood; so that a farmer who comes upon the eggs will know and will be able to tell others just how far the river will rise. Her purpose in being so exact is that neither she nor the eggs will get wet when she is incubating them. And when the young crocodiles are hatched, any one of them which, on emerging from the egg, fails to snap up immediately in its jaws whatever comes along – fly, worm, straw or plant – will be bitten to death and torn to pieces by its mother; but she shows great affection and gives great care to those which show courage and energy. Her love is thus determined by judgement, not by emotion, which is just what the wisest among us recommend.

Seals also give birth on dry land. From here they encourage their young little by little to try the taste of the sea and then quickly take them out of it. They do this over and over again until the young have got used to the salt water and feel confidence so that they enjoy life in the sea.

When frogs are mating, they make use of a call – the ololygon, as we call it – which is a kind of love or marriage song. When the male has won over the female in this way, they wait together until nightfall, since they cannot mate in the water and are afraid to do so on land during the day; but when it is dark they come out and copulate without fear. At other times they make their voices shrill. This is when they expect rain and it is among the surest signs that rain is on the way.

35. But, dear Poseidon! How close I have come to making an utter fool of myself! Here I am going on talking about seals and frogs and meanwhile the wisest of all sea creatures and the one the gods love best has quite slipped out of my mind! Now where are the nightingales which can be compared with the halcyon for love of music? Where are the swallows for love of children, or the doves for love of their mates or the bees for technology? Where is there another creature who at the time of birth and when the pangs of labour are upon her receives such honour from heaven? We are told that, when Leto was about to give birth, only one island was anchored in the sea to receive her; but when the halcyon lays her eggs, about the time of the winter solstice, Poseidon makes the whole sea calm; there is no swell, there is no wave. And this is why there is no creature which men love more than the halcyon. Thanks to her they have seven days and seven nights at the very height of winter during which they can sail the sea without fear, and for this period indeed it is safer to travel by sea than by land.

And, if I may say a few words about her various virtues, her love for her husband is such that she lives with him and will cohabit with him not just for a single season, but all through the year. This is not because of any lack of self-control, for she will never have anything to do with any other male; it is from good feeling and affection, as with any married woman. And when the male grows old and becomes too weak and slow to keep up with her, she takes upon herself the burden of carrying and feeding him in his old age. Never forsaking him, never parting from him, she takes him up on her shoulders and carries him with her wherever she goes, caring for him and staying with him to the end.

I come next to the love she shows for her children and the

care she takes for their preservation. As soon as she realizes that she is pregnant, she starts work on the building of her nest. And for this she does not make a mixture of mud and plaster it on walls and roofs, like the house-martin; nor does she use a number of different parts of her body for getting the work done, as bees do when they thrust the whole of their bodies into the wax to open it up and use all six feet simultaneously to press and shape it all into hexagonal cells. The halcyon has only one simple tool, one implement, one piece of equipment – her beak, and only her beak. But with this and with her delight in hard work and in technology she designs and builds a structure which would be almost unbelievable unless one had actually seen the fabric she makes or, one might say, the ship she builds. This could have been shaped in a number of different ways, but the shape she has selected is the only one which cannot be capsized and cannot even let the water in. She collects the spines of garfish and binds and weaves them together, some upright, some transverse, just as if she were weaving on a loom; and she goes on to bend and tighten it up with knots so as to form one rounded hull, slightly oblong, like a fisherman's creel. When it is finished she carries it to the edge of the sea where the waves are breaking and sets it down there and, as the water washes gently on it, she observes where it is loosened by the action of the waves, and learns how to repair and strengthen any part which is not yet firmly and properly fitted. And she tightens up the joints and makes everything fast so that the nest could scarcely be broken or damaged even by stones or iron. The proportions and shape of the hollow interior are as wonderful as anything else. It is so constructed that only the halcyon herself can enter it and the entrance is entirely hidden and invisible to others, so that not a single drop of water can get in.

I'm sure that all of you have seen this nest. I myself have

seen it often and held it in my hands and now it occurs to me
to recite the words:

Once such a thing in Delos, beside the shrine of Apollo [57]
I saw, namely the Altar of Horn which is renowned as one
of the Seven Wonders of the World, because it needs no
glue or anything else to keep it altogether; it is firmly
compacted together and made entirely of horns taken from
the right side of the head.

Now let the god look kindly on me while I sing of the
Sea Siren, and since Apollo is both a musician and an islander,
he can be expected to laugh, though quite good-naturedly,
at my opponents for mocking me with such questions as
'Why is Apollo not called conger-slayer or Artemis mullet-
slayer?' Apollo knows well enough that Aphrodite, who was
born of the sea, regards practically all sea-creatures as sacred
and as her own relations, and that she takes no pleasure in the
slaughter of any of them. You know that at Leptis the priests
of Poseidon will not eat any sea food and that those who are
initiated into the mysteries of Eleusis regard the surmullet as
sacred; the priestess of Hera at Argos also honours this fish
and abstains from its flesh. Surmullets are particularly good at
killing and eating the sea-hare, which is lethal to man; and
this is why they are given this immunity, since they are the
friends and preservers of man.

36. In fact many Greek cities have temples and altars
dedicated to Artemis Dictynna and Apollo Delphinios. [58] And
the poet [59] tells us that the place chosen by the god for himself
was settled by Cretans who were guided there by a dolphin.
According to the story tellers the god changed his shape and
himself swam in front of the party; but this is not so. What

57. Homer, *Odyssey*, 6. 162.
58. As it were 'Artemis of the Nets', 'Apollo of the Dolphin'.
59. Homer, *Hymn 3 (To Apollo)*, 393 ff.

he did was to send a dolphin to show the way and guide the men into the port of Cirrha.[60]

We are also told that when Sotele and Dionysius were sent to Sinope by Ptolemy Soter to bring back Serapis,[61] they were forced off their course by a violent storm and driven beyond Malea with the Peloponnese on their right. They were completely lost and dispirited when a dolphin appeared by the ship's prow, as it were inviting them to follow him. And so he led them on to places with safe anchorages where there was very little swell and continued to guide and escort them until he had brought them to the port of Cirrha. And so it happened that, when they had offered thanksgiving for their safe landing, they were instructed that of the two statues they should take away the one of Pluto, but should leave at Sinope the statue of Persephone, after taking an impression of it.

It was natural enough that Apollo should be pleased with the dolphin's love of music. Pindar also compares himself to the dolphin when he says that he is stirred up:

> As a dolphin of the sea
> Who in waveless depths of ocean
> Is moved by lovely melody of flutes.[62]

But it is even more natural that what makes it dear to the gods is its affection for man. It is the only creature who loves man for himself. But land animals either want nothing to do with man at all or, in the case of the tamest ones, such as dogs, horses and elephants, the consideration they show is a matter of self-interest and is confined to those who feed them and with whom they are familiar. Martins come to our homes to get what they need, darkness and the security they have to

60. The port of Delphi.
61. cf. Tacitus, *Histories*, 4. 83–4.
62. Fr. 140b, 15–17.

have; but they avoid and fear man as though he were a wild beast. But the dolphin stands by himself; to him alone nature has given what all the best philosophers seek – love which is disinterested. The dolphin has no need of anything from any man, yet he is a good friend to all and has come to the help of many. The story of Arion[63] is so well known that everyone has heard it. And you, my friend, came in very aptly with the story of Hesiod.[64]

But failed to finish the story.[65]

When you were telling us about the dog, you ought not to have left out the dolphins. The information provided by the dog howling and barking and rushing at the murderers would have meant nothing at all had it not been for the dolphins which recovered the corpse floating in the sea near the Nemeon and willingly came up in relays to carry it and put it down on the shore at Rhium so as to show that the man had indeed been stabbed.

Myrsilus of Lesbos tells how Enalus the Aeolian was in love with the daughter of Smintheus. In obedience to the oracle of Amphitrite she was thrown into the sea by the Penthelidae, upon which Enalus himself leaped into the sea from which he was brought out by a dolphin and put safe ashore on Lesbos.

And the kindness and friendship shown by the dolphin to the boy of Iasus was so great that it has been considered an example of really passionate love. Every day it used to swim about and play with him and would let him touch it. Then, when the boy mounted on its back, it was perfectly willing and would gladly carry him wherever he steered it; and all the inhabitants of Iasus would flock to the shore whenever

63. cf. Herodotus, *History*, 1. 24.
64. cf. above, p. 122, 969 E.
65. Homer, *Iliad*, 9. 56.

this was going on. But on one occasion there was a great storm of rain and hail and the boy slipped off and was drowned. The dolphin recovered the body and threw both it and himself on land and would not leave it until he too had died. He considered that he was partly to blame for the boy's death and thought it only right that he should share his fate. In memory of this sad event the people of Iasus have their coins engraved with the figure of a boy riding a dolphin.

Because of this true story people believe the stories about Coeranus, fanciful as they are. He was a Parian by birth, and at Byzantium he bought a catch of dolphins that had been netted and were likely to be killed and set them all free. A little later he was sailing in a penteconter which they say had fifty pirates aboard. The ship capsized in the strait between Naxos and Paros and everyone was drowned except for Coeranus, who was rescued by a dolphin which rushed up from beneath, buoyed him up and put him ashore at Sicinus near a cave which is still pointed out and is called the cave of Coeranus. It is about him that Archilochus is said to have written the line.

Kind Poseidon out of fifty men saved Coeranus alone.[66]

Later, when Coeranus died, and his family were burning the body by the sea, a large school of dolphins appeared close to the beach as though they wanted to show that they had come for the funeral and they did not go away until it was over.

Stesichorus tells us that Odysseus had a dolphin emblazoned on his shield and the reason for this, according to Critheus, has been preserved in the traditions of the people of Zacynthus. They say that when Telemachus was a small boy he fell into some deep water near the shore and was saved by dolphins who came to his help and swam with him to the beach.

66. Fr. 177, in E. Diehl (ed.), *Anthologia Lyrica Graeca*, 3rd ed., Leipzig, 1949–52.

And so in gratitude to these creatures his father had a dolphin engraved on his ring and emblazoned on his shield.

But I promised you at the beginning that I was not going to tell you any fairy stories, and now on this subject of dolphins I seem, without knowing it, to have run aground on the reefs of incredibility with these stories of Odysseus and Coeranus. Well, I'll fix the penalty for myself. I'll end my speech and say no more.

37. ARISTOTIMUS: And now, gentlemen of the jury, you may cast your votes.

SOCLARUS: For some time now we have been appreciating the justice of what Sophocles says:

> How well the argument on either side
> Sticks and combines together in a common ground.[67]

For if one brings together what you have said, speaking in opposition, the two of you together will put up a very good fight against those who say that animals are without reason and understanding.

67. Fr. 783.

Odysseus and Gryllus

* *
*

INTRODUCTORY NOTE

THIS dialogue has a mythological setting, like some of Lucian's. Plutarch imagines Circe introducing Odysseus to an ex-man, now happy as a pig. Moral themes – simplicity of life, kindness, avoidance of luxury – are handled in an entertaining and lively way; this is unusual Plutarch, but obviously successful.

The speakers are Odysseus, Circe and Grunter (Gryllus).

1. ODYSSEUS: Well, Circe, I think that I have grasped what you have told me and shall not forget it. But there is something else which I should be glad to know. Have you got any Greeks among these creatures who used to be men but whom you have changed into wolves and lions?

CIRCE: Oh yes, darling Odysseus, quite a lot. But why do you want to know?

ODYSSEUS: To speak frankly, I think it would do me very great credit among my countrymen if you would be so kind as to allow me to rescue my old comrades and make them human again and not let them grow old in these unnatural shapes, living such a sad life, and so dishonourable.

CIRCE: My dear man, what stupidity! I suppose you think it quite all right that this love of honour of yours should bring disaster, not only to yourself and your friends, but to perfect strangers as well.

ODYSSEUS: Is this another magic drug, my dear Circe, that you are concocting for me in this argument? Sure

159

enough it would really turn me into a beast if I were to believe you when you say that it is a disaster to be a man rather than a beast.

CIRCE: Personally I'd say that you'd already doped yourself to a much more absurd degree than that. Haven't you refused to live with me ageless and immortal, and aren't you eager to be off into more and more dangers in order to get back to a woman who is mortal and who must be, I can tell you, getting on in years by now? And all this simply to make yourself famous for it and even better known than you are already! What you are doing is just chasing after an empty shadow instead of reality.

ODYSSEUS: Have it your own way, Circe. There is really no point in always quarrelling about the same thing. But do, please, just be so kind as to let these men go.

CIRCE: By Hecate, it's not so easy. These are not ordinary creatures at all. What you must do is to ask first if they want to become men again. And if they don't want to, you must argue with them, my hero, and persuade them. But perhaps you won't persuade them; perhaps they will come out on top in the argument. And then you'll have to admit that your judgement about yourself and your friends wasn't very good.

ODYSSEUS: My sweet Circe, why are you laughing at me? How can they and I hold any conversation at all so long as they remain asses and pigs and lions?

CIRCE: Don't lose heart, my man of honour. I'll arrange things so that they can understand you and say what they want to. Or wouldn't it be better to have just one of them to speak and answer for all the rest? Here you are. Talk to this one.

ODYSSEUS: But what shall I call him, Circe? Who was he when he was a man?

CIRCE: What difference does that make? But call him

'Grunter' if you like. And I'll go right out of the way so that there'll be no chance of his saying anything he doesn't mean in order to make himself popular with me.

2. GRUNTER: How do you do, Odysseus?

ODYSSEUS: And how do you do, Grunter?

GRUNTER: What is it you want to ask?

ODYSSEUS: I have come to know that you were once men and I feel very sorry for you all in your present condition. But it's only natural that I should be still more concerned for those of you who were Greeks before this terrible thing happened to you. So now I have asked Circe to set free any Greek who chooses and to restore him to his original shape and let him come back with us.

GRUNTER: Odysseus, stop! No more, please! The fact is that none of us has a very high opinion of you. It was all nonsense, it seems, that talk about how clever you were and how you were considered so much more intelligent than anyone else. And now we find that the thing which really frightens you (and without having looked into the matter at all) is a change from the worse to the better. You are like a child frightened of the doctor's medicine or running away from his lessons – just the things which will make him healthy instead of sick, wise instead of a fool. So you dread the change from one shape to another. Meanwhile you yourself are living with Circe in a constant state of abject terror in case, before you know what's happened, she may turn you into a pig or a wolf; and now you come and try to persuade us, who have all the good things we want, to give them all up, to abandon Circe who provides us with them, and to sail away with you, reverting again to the condition of man, the most miserable thing alive.

ODYSSEUS: It's my impression, Grunter, that that drug you took has made you lose your intelligence as well as your shape, and filled you up with a lot of absurd and absolutely perverted ideas. Or was it a natural pleasure in swinishness that charmed you into this shape?

GRUNTER: Neither of the two, King of the Cephalonians.[1] But if you want a reasonable discussion rather than a slanging match, I shall soon make you change your mind and see that we, who have had experience of both ways of life, very properly prefer the life we have now to the one which we used to have.

ODYSSEUS: Go ahead. I'm always delighted to learn.

GRUNTER: And I'm quite willing to teach. Let us start with virtue. This is something, we observe, of which you are very proud, since you consider yourselves greatly superior to animals in justice, wisdom, courage and all the rest. Well, answer me this from your great wisdom. I heard you once telling Circe about the land of the Cyclopes[2] and saying that though it is never ploughed or sown it is naturally such good fertile land that it produces every kind of crop of its own accord. Now which do you put first, the land of the Cyclopes or your own rocky, goat-pasturing Ithaca[3] out of which the farmer, work and toil as he may, can scarcely get even a wretched, miserable and worthless yield? And please don't get angry and patriotically say something you don't really mean.

ODYSSEUS: There's no need for me to tell a lie. I feel more love and affection for my own country and my own soil, but I think that the land of the Cyclopes is better and more admirable.

GRUNTER: Shall we say that this is how the matter stands? The wisest of men gives his love and preference to one thing, while admitting that another thing is better and more worthwhile? And I think I may assume that you would give the

1. *Perhaps* a pun is intended: 'king of brains' (*kephalē* = head).
2. *Odyssey*, 9. 108 ff.
3. ibid., 13. 242 ff.

same answer with regard to spiritual matters, since here the same rule holds good as with the soil: the best spiritual soil is the one that yields a harvest of virtue naturally and without hard labour.

ODYSSEUS: Yes, I will grant you this too.

GRUNTER: Then you have already admitted that animals have souls that are more naturally and perfectly disposed to produce virtue than men have. The soul of an animal needs no commandments, no education; 'unsown and unploughed' as you might say, it bears and brings to maturity quite naturally the right virtue in the right place.

ODYSSEUS: Virtue, Grunter? What sort of virtue can animals have?

GRUNTER: It would be more sensible to ask if there is any virtue in which they are not superior to the wisest man you can find. Let us start, if you like, with courage. This is something which you are very proud of yourself and you are not at all averse from hearing yourself described as 'brave Odysseus' or 'sacker of cities'.[4] Yet it is you who are the villain of the piece. The only style of warfare that men used to know was honourable and straightforward; they knew nothing of treachery and deceit until you led them astray with your stratagems and your modern weapons. Virtue is absolutely incompatible with lack of scruple; yet you call your unscrupulousness virtue. But, as you can see, there is nothing treacherous or artful about animals when they are fighting with each other or against you; the courage with which they defend themselves is pure courage and nothing else, and when they are brave, they are really brave. They are not conscripted under any law, nor are they afraid of being persecuted for desertion; it is their nature to refuse to submit and they will endure to the end without ever giving in. They may be physically overpowered, but their spirit is still unbroken and

4. e.g. *Iliad*, 2. 278.

they will die fighting. Often when an animal is actually dying, its courage and fighting spirit will become concentrated and withdraw to just one part of the body which will still fight back with angry convulsive movements against the man who is killing it until, finally, this too is put out like a flame and disappears.

Animals never beg, never ask for pity, never surrender. A lion does not become a slave to another lion through cowardice, nor a horse to a horse, as man becomes slave to man and is perfectly happy to be called by a name which is derived from the word for cowardice.[5]

And when by means of traps and other deceitful methods men succeed in getting animals into their power, the full grown ones will refuse food and endure the pangs of thirst to bring on death, since they prefer death to slavery. Nestlings and cubs, on the other hand, are tender and easily led because of their age, so men drug them by offering them all kinds of treacherous dainties and appetizers which give them a taste for unnatural pleasures and an unnatural way of life, and end up by making them spiritless so that they will accept and submit to what we call 'being tamed' – which means, of course, being emasculated, so far as their fighting spirit is concerned.

These facts make it perfectly clear that animals are courageous and independent by nature. Among human beings, on the other hand, independence is actually unnatural. The best example I can give you of this, my dear Odysseus, is in the fact that among animals each sex is naturally as brave as the other; the female is in no way inferior to the male. She takes her share in all the work that has to be done and also in fighting in defence of their brood. No doubt you've heard of the

5. Another of Plutarch's odd derivations. *Douleia* (slavery) is supposed to be derived from *deilia* (cowardice).

sow of Crommyon.[6] She was female, but she gave Theseus a good deal of trouble. And the famous Sphinx, sitting up on the rocks of Phicium and weaving her riddles and conundrums, would not have got far with all her wisdom if she had not also been far superior to the Thebans in power and courage. Somewhere in the neighbourhood there was also living that 'baleful thing', the Teumesian vixen;[7] and not far off, they say, was the Pythoness who fought with Apollo for the oracle at Delphi. Your king[8] got his mare, Aethe, from Echepolus of Sicyon as a bribe for getting out of military service. And here Agamemnon was extremely sensible to choose a fine spirited mare rather than a cowardly man.

You yourself have often seen in the case of panthers and lions that the female is just as courageous and as fierce as the male. But what about your wife, Penelope? While you are away at the war, she sits at home by the fire and does about as much as a swallow might do to get rid of the young men who want to lay hold on her and the property – and this though she is Spartan born and bred. So why should I go on to say anything about what the women in Caria or Maeonia[9] are like?

Surely it must be clear from all this that courage is not something implanted in man by nature. If it were, women would be as brave as men are. So you have to be trained in courage and this training is not voluntary or self imposed; it is forced on you by law and convention which enslaves you to custom and the fear of what others may think, and which is all made up of beliefs and arguments that come from out-

6. cf. Plutarch, *Life of Theseus*, 9.

7. Meant by Dionysus to ravage Theban territory, but turned into a stone at the moment of capture by a dog given to Procris by Artemis (Pausanias, 9. 19. 1).

8. *Iliad*, 23. 295–9.

9. Proverbially effeminate countries as Sparta is proverbially virile.

side. When you stand up to difficulties and dangers, it is not because you have the courage to confront them but because you are still more afraid of something else. It's like when you and your comrades are embarking and the first man aboard seizes hold of the light oar. He does this not because hard work means nothing to him but because he's scared stiff of getting one of the heavier oars. And so with the man who will take a blow rather than a sword-thrust or who will fight against an enemy rather than be tortured or killed; what he shows is not courage in the face of one situation so much as fear in the face of the other. It is evident, then, that with you to be brave means simply to be cowardly in an intelligent way, and courage is merely fear with enough sense to escape one alternative by choosing the other.

Finally, if you really think that you are superior to animals in courage, how does it come about that your poets describe your mightiest warriors as 'fierce as a wolf', and 'lion-hearted' and 'brave as a boar'? Has any poet ever called a lion 'man-hearted', or a boar 'brave as a man'? As I see it, the same principle of exaggerated imagery is involved here as when we call speedy runners 'fast as the wind' or handsome people 'godlike'. In just the same way the poets compare men who are good at fighting to something which is still better at it. And the reason why animals are better is this: it is the quick impulse of anger that gives courage its sharp edge and its final tempering, and animals have this quality in all its purity when they go to battle, whereas you men, as though you were watering down your wine, blend it with calculation; and the result is that it disappears in the face of danger and leaves you just when you need it. Some of you even say that there is no place at all for impulsive anger in fighting and that it should be replaced by sober calculation. And so far as self-preservation is concerned, no doubt they are quite right; but it is a disgraceful view to hold, if one is thinking in terms of leaping into action against the enemy. Is it not rather absurd of you to blame nature for not having furnished your bodies with stings or tusks or claws, while you yourselves either get rid of or blunt this weapon of impulse which she did implant in your souls?

ODYSSEUS: Really, Grunter, I think that you must have once been a brilliant sophist. It's remarkable how even now in spite of your swinishness you deal so beautifully and enthusiastically with your subject. But why haven't you gone on to the next of the virtues, temperance?

GRUNTER: I thought you might like to raise some objections to what I've just said. But I see that you are eager to hear about temperance, no doubt because you are the husband of a paragon of chastity and you fancy you have given an exhibition of self-control yourself in not being swept off your feet by Circe's love. Actually you show no more self-control here than does any animal. Animals also have no desire to mix with their betters; for pleasure and for love they confine themselves to their own species. They tell us that the Mendesian goat in Egypt, if he is shut up with any number of beautiful women, is not at all eager to copulate with them and is much more excited by female goats. So it is not at all surprising that you too should enjoy the love to which you are used and, being a mortal, should be reluctant to go to bed with a goddess. And as for Penelope's chastity, every female crow in the world would caw with laughter and contempt at it; for every crow, if her mate dies, remains a widow, not just for a short time but for nine human generations. So any crow you choose is nine times chaster than your wonderful Penelope.

6. However, since you seem to have discovered that I am a sophist, let me bring some sort of order into my argument. I shall first define temperance, and then analyse the specific desires which we feel. Temperance, then, is a kind of cutting

down and setting in order of desires. Some desires are foreign to our nature and unnecessary, others are necessary; it gets rid of the former altogether and it regulates the latter with a due regard for moderation in time and place. You can, of course, observe all kinds of difference in desires; for the desire for food and drink is both natural and necessary, whereas though the pleasures of sex certainly originate from nature one can do without them and give them up without too much trouble, and so they have been called natural, but not necessary. But there are also desires which are neither natural nor necessary; they come from outside in vast numbers and thrive on the absurd illusions into which you fall because of your ignorance of what is really good, and they have so overwhelmed you as pretty well to do away with every natural desire; it is as though a horde of foreigners had invaded and was over-running the native population. But these extraneous and imported emotions can find no sort of entry into the souls of animals, who live their lives as remote from such commerce as if they were settled far from the sea. No doubt they are behind you in luxury and extravagant living; on the other hand they keep a very good guard on their modesty and are the better able to govern their desires because there are not many of them and these are not of foreign origin.

I admit that I was once as you are now. I was dazzled by gold and thought it an incomparable possession; I was enchanted by silver and ivory. I thought that whoever had most of these was favoured by the gods and ideally happy, though he might be a Phrygian or a Carian, more treacherous than Dolon[10] or more unfortunate than Priam. In that state of mind and governed by these desires I was kept dangling in the air and could find no joy or delight in all the other things of which I had enough and to spare. I was in constant

10. A Trojan spy; see *Iliad*, 10.

discontent, imagining that I lacked what really mattered and that I had been left without my share in the good things of life. This was why, I remember, when I saw you in Crete[11] all dressed up for a public occasion, what I envied about you was not your intellect or your good qualities. No, it was the softness of your finely woven tunic that I was admiring and gaping at and the lovely wool of your purple cloak (it had a gold clasp, I think, with some trivial kind of subject worked on it in intaglio). I was bewitched by this and followed you about like a woman. But now I'm free and purified of these empty illusions; gold and silver I pass by without looking at, like any other stone. And as for your blankets and coverlets, I swear that I like nothing better when I'm full than going to sleep in some deep soft mud. Not one of this class of imported desires has a place in our hearts. Most of our life is controlled by those desires which are necessary to existence and as for those which are natural, but not necessary, we indulge in them with a due regard for priorities and for moderation.

7. Let us first of all examine what these pleasures are. The pleasure that we find in sweet smelling things that naturally give out a scent that stimulates our sense of smell is a pleasure which, apart from being simple and costing nothing, is positively useful, since it enables us to tell good food from bad. The tongue is supposed to be our guide for what is sweet or bitter or sour and this is quite true once the flavours blend and liquefy and so act on the organs of taste; but even before we have tasted a thing, our sense of smell can distinguish and evaluate its various qualities much more efficiently than those whose job it is to taste the food served to kings. It welcomes what is good for us and rejects what is not and instead of letting anything come in disagreeable contact with our taste, it gives us damning information of its badness

11. *Odyssey*, 19. 225 ff.

before any harm is done. Nor does our sense of smell give us any trouble as it does with you by forcing you to lay in great stores of various kinds of incense and cinnamon and nard and malobathrum and scented reeds from Arabia, and then with the help of colour-blending and sorcery – which you call the great art of perfumery – to mix them all up together and so acquire at enormous expense a luxury which is unmanly and schoolgirlish and of absolutely no use at all. Yet, useless as it is, it has corrupted all women and by this time most men too, so that they won't sleep even with their own wives unless they come to bed reeking of perfume and face powder. But sows attract boars and she goats attract he goats and other female creatures attract their mates by the smell they naturally have; their scent is that of pure dew and grass meadows and they come together because of mutual affection. The females are not coy and don't hide their desires behind pretences and oglings and denials; nor do the males, driven mad and crazy by their lusts, pay for the act of procreation with hard cash or hard labour or servile behaviour. The love they seek and find is given freely and sincerely and at the proper time. Just as the flowers and trees come out in spring in leaves and blossoms, so the desire of animals springs up and then immediately dies down. Once the female has conceived, she will no longer admit the male nor will he try to force himself on her. Mere pleasure means very little indeed to us; with us Nature is everything. This is why up to the present day the desires of animals have never led them into Lesbian or homosexual practices. You, on the other hand, have a lot of this and one finds it not only among the lowest types but among the aristocracy and the most respectable people. Agamemnon came to Boeotia chasing after Argynnus who was trying to escape him.[12] He slandered the sea and the winds, and then this wonderful man had a wonderful bath in Lake Copais to

12. See Propertius, 3. 7. 21.

quench his passion and get rid of his desire. So Heracles too in his search for his smooth-cheeked boy friend[13] got left behind by the other heroes[14] and let down the whole expedition. And on the Rotunda of Ptoian Apollo one of your men, when no one was looking, inscribed the words 'Achilles is beautiful' – and this when Achilles was already a father. And I hear that the inscription is still there. But a cock that, for lack of a hen, mounts another cock is burned alive because some prophet or sooth-sayer tells us that such a thing is likely to have terribly important consequences. From this kind of reasoning it would appear that men themselves admit that it is more normal for animals to be temperate and to avoid being led astray by pleasure into unnatural acts than it is for them. As for you men, even when Nature has the laws on her side to help her, your debauchery still cannot be kept within bounds. Carried away by your desires, you are constantly doing violence to nature in your sexual practices, subverting the order and blurring the distinctions which nature has laid down. Men have actually practised bestiality with goats and sows and mares, and women have gone mad with lust for male animals. No doubt it was from this sort of thing that there arose your Minotaurs and Satyrs and Sphinxes and Centaurs. But if a dog does ever eat a man it is because of hunger, and birds only taste human flesh from necessity. No animal has ever wanted to make use of a human body for reasons of sexuality. Animals, on the other hand (both those I have mentioned and many others), have often been exposed to the violent and outrageous lusts of men.

8. The vice and incontinence of men with regard to the particular type of desires which we have been discussing are

13. Heracles pursued Hylas, who was dragged down into a pool by nymphs. A favourite Alexandrian subject: Theocritus 13; Apollonius Rhodius, 1. 1207ff.

14. The Argonauts.

evident enough; but they can easily be shown to be even more greatly inferior to animals in temperance with regard to those other desires, which we called necessary. These are the desires for food and drink and here we animals always combine pleasure with utility. You, on the other hand, put pleasure first and the nourishment required by nature second, and as a result you suffer from all sorts of serious illnesses which all stem from one source, over-indulgence, which fills you with all sorts of stomach gases of which you can't get rid. In the first place, each species of animal has one particular food which is natural to it; some eat grass, others some kind of root or fruit. And those which are carnivorous eat this kind of food alone and no other; they do not deprive those weaker than themselves of their food; the lion lets the deer and the wolf lets the sheep feed in their own natural way. But man's pleasure is so involved with gluttony that everything attracts him; he will try everything and taste everything just as if he still didn't know what was good for him; he is the only omnivorous creature in the world.

Why, in the first place, does he eat flesh? It is not because of any lack of other food or any inability to procure it. Vegetables and cereals are always available to him in season, one after another, and he can harvest and store and pick them in such quantities that the very labour of doing so would tire him out. But his taste is for luxury; necessary and wholesome food disgusts him; and so he must slaughter animals and take to food which is both unnatural and useless. And here he shows more heartlessness than any wild beast. For kites and wolves and snakes, blood and entrails and raw flesh are the normal and natural diet. For man they are just appetizers. Then, too, man makes use of every kind of creature there is for food, whereas animals abstain from all except a few which they hunt because they have to have nourishment. But with you there is practically nothing that flies or swims or moves on land that has escaped what you like to call your civilized tables and your gracious style of living.

9. All right. You may say that you use these appetizers to make your food go down better. Then why . . .?[15] Animal intelligence, on the other hand, allows no scope for skills that are useless and pointless, and our essential skills do not have to be imported from outside nor do we pay to learn them; we do not force one individual to stick to one special subject and never go outside his department; with us the appropriate skills are natural and inborn and can be called upon immediately. I have heard that in Egypt everyone is a physician; but among animals each one of us is an expert not only in medicine but also in economics, in warfare, in hunting, in defence and in those branches of higher learning to which we may be naturally adapted. Did anyone teach us pigs to go to rivers to catch crabs when we feel sick? Did anyone teach tortoises to take marjoram after eating a snake? Did anyone teach the goats in Crete, when wounded by an arrow, to look for dittany, after eating which the arrowhead falls out? If you tell the truth, you will say that the teacher is Nature, and will grant that animal intelligence is based on the surest and wisest of first principles. And if you don't think that reason or intelligence are the proper words to use for it, it is high time for you to look around for some other word of even greater lustre and distinction, since there is no doubt at all that its final result in action is better and more wonderful than anything you can manage. Nor can you call this faculty of ours uneducated or untrained; it is self-educated and self-sufficient, and this not because of any weakness, but because of the vigour and the perfection of a virtue that is natural and that can afford to be indifferent to any intellectual contribution that might

15. There is a lacuna here. The sense may be: 'Then why do you have to invent a special art of cookery? Animal intelligence, on the other hand . . .'

be made by other people's learning. Certainly when we look at those animals which men, for amusement and for self-indulgence have induced to take lessons and undergo training, we observe that their intelligence is so great that they can grasp and understand what they are taught even when it is something that is quite contrary to their natural powers. I'll say nothing about young dogs that are trained for hunting, or colts that are taught to go through their various paces, or crows taught to talk, or dogs to jump through spinning hoops. But think of the horses and bullocks we see in shows and how they learn and memorize most complicated sets of tricks involving lying down, dancing, balancing acts, and various movements which even men find difficult; and these exhibitions of docility which they give are of no practical use at all.

And if you are in any doubt about our ability to learn the arts, then let me tell you that we can actually teach them. When partridges are flying out of the way of danger, they train their young to take cover by falling on their backs and holding a bit of earth over themselves with their claws. And you can see on the roof tops how the adult storks stand by and instruct the young storks in their first attempts at flight. Nightingales too train their young to imitate their song. The ones who are caught in the nest and brought up by man do not sing so well, just as though they had been taken away too soon from school . . .[16] and since I have been in this present body of mine, I have been astounded when I think of those arguments by which the sophists induced me to believe that all creatures except man are irrational and senseless.

10. ODYSSEUS: Well, Grunter, now that you have changed your shape are you going to say that even sheep and asses have reason?

GRUNTER: Certainly, my dear Odysseus. In fact it's just here that you'll find the clearest proof of the presence of

16. There is probably a long lacuna here.

reason and intellect in animal nature. You can't say that one tree is more or less inanimate than another, and must grant that they are all in the same state of insensibility, since none of them has a soul. Well, in just the same way, it would not be possible to think of one animal as mentally more sluggish and harder to teach than another, if it were not true that all animals do have reason and intellect in some degree – though some have more and some less of it than others. Remember that what makes us call some animals dull and stupid is the fact that other animals are clever and quick – when, for instance, you compare a sheep with a fox or a wolf or a bee. It's like comparing Polyphemus with you, or that fool Coroebus[17] with your grandfather Autolycus.[18] I don't think, in fact, that there is such a big difference between one animal and another as there is between one man and another man in such things as judgement, reasoning powers and memory.

ODYSSEUS: But, Grunter, think of this: is there not something rather monstrous about assuming that reason can exist in creatures which have no knowledge of God?

GRUNTER: But then, Odysseus, we shall have to say that such a remarkably clever man as you are couldn't have been descended from Sisyphus.[19]

17. He was foolish enough to try to count the waves.

18. *Odyssey*, 19. 394 ff.

19. Many critics believe that the end of this dialogue has been lost and that there must have been a more or less lengthy discussion of the other virtues. Some, however, may feel that the present ending is both witty and appropriate. Certainly Grunter has made a good point. Odysseus is pre-eminently gifted with reason; yet his ancestor (i.e. in some versions, his father) Sisyphus certainly had no knowledge of God, or at least not till after death, since he did not believe the gods existed.

A Letter of Consolation to his Wife on the Death of an Infant Daughter

* *
*

INTRODUCTORY NOTE

THE evidence concerning Plutarch's family is confusing, but the circumstances of this piece are plain. His infant daughter Timoxena has died; he is away from home, and writes a letter of comfort to his wife. Despite its literary tone and ready use of commonplaces, the letter is a moving and sincere document, typical of Plutarch, and rightly much admired.

1. *To my wife, all good wishes.*

The messenger you sent to tell me about the death of our little daughter seems to have missed me on the road on his way to Athens. But when I got to Tanagra I heard what had happened from my grand-daughter.

I expect that the funeral is now over, and I do hope that everything was done in the way that would cause you the least pain both now and for the future. But if there is anything which you would like to have done and which you have not had done, because you were waiting for my approval – anything, I mean, which you think would make your grief easier to bear, please see that that is done too. I know that there will be no question of any ostentation or any superstition, because these are not faults to which you are at all liable.

2. Only, my dear wife, you must try to think of me as well as yourself in your sorrow and to keep us both steady. I know what a great loss we have had and I can take the measure of

it; but if I find you utterly overwhelmed by grief, I shall find this even harder to bear than what has happened. And yet I was not born 'from oak or rock'.[1] You know that yourself, since you and I together have had many children and we have brought all of them up at home and looked after them ourselves. And I know how wonderfully happy we were when, after four sons, the daughter whom you had always longed to have was born and so made it possible for me to give your name to one of our children.

Then too there is a very special kind of poignancy about the love we feel for such very young children; it is an absolutely pure pleasure undisturbed by anything like anger or blame. And our little girl had such a wonderfully good and kind nature; and the way she had of loving those who loved her and of doing kindnesses to others not only gave us pleasure but enabled us to see what a good heart she had. You remember how she would get her nurse to offer her breast and feed not only other small children but even the toys and playthings she was fond of; it was as though she were inviting them to her own table, hospitably entertaining them with all the good things she had and sharing her greatest pleasures with all things that made her happy.

3. But, my dear wife, I do not see why these things about her which so delighted us when she was alive should pain and distress us when we think of them now. On the contrary what I am more afraid of is that pain suppressed will lead to loss of memory, as with Clymene, when she says:

> I hate the crooked bow
> Of cornel wood, all young men's sports. Let them be gone![2]

Here she is constantly avoiding and shrinking from whatever could remind her of her son, since the memory brought pain

1. Homer, *Iliad*, 22. 126; *Odyssey*, 19. 163.
2. From the *Phaethon* of Euripides, fr. 785.

with it; and nature shrinks from everything unpleasant. But we must not be like that. Just as it was the sweetest thing in the world for us to hold her in our arms and look at her and listen to her, so now the thought of her must live with us and share our lives, and bring us more joy, much more joy, than sorrow (if it is at all reasonable that the arguments which we have often used to other people should be of help to us too in our hour of need). We must not just sit still and hide ourselves away, paying for those pleasures with a far greater quantity of pain.

4. I heard too from those who were with you at the time – and they were amazed at it – that you have not even put on mourning, that you didn't force yourself or any of the maids to behave in any unsightly or unbecoming way and that at the funeral there was no extravagance and none of that display, which is better suited to a feast; instead everything was done properly and quietly with just our relations present. This, of course, did not surprise me. You were never one to over-dress when going to the theatre or to a procession and regarded extravagance as a useless thing even for amusements. So I was not surprised that on this sad occasion, too, your quiet and modest ways were just the same. It is not only in 'the rites of Bacchus'[3] that the virtuous woman should stay uncorrupted; she should recognize that in the storm and stress of the emotion of grief just as much self-control is required, and this self-control does not mean suppressing, as most people think, her feelings as a mother; it does mean suppressing the self-indulgent element in the mind. When we long for and honour and remember the departed we are gratifying our normal parental feelings; but the insatiable passion for lamentation, which drives people to weeping and wailing and beating the breast, is just as disgraceful as unrestrained indulgence in pleasure. It gets excused on the grounds that sorrow and

3. cf. Euripides, *Bacchae*, 371 f.

pain rather than pleasure are behind the disgracefulness of the conduct, but the excuse is not a convincing one. Is it not absurd to ban excessive laughter and displays of joy and then to allow free play to those torrents of weeping and wailing that come from just the same source? Is it not absurd for people to quarrel with their wives about using perfume or dressing in purple and then to allow them to cut their hair off as a sign of mourning, to dye their clothes black, to sit down in ungainly positions and to lie down in uncomfortable ones? Worse still, to protest against their wives and stop them if they are punishing their servants or maids unjustly and unnecessarily, but not to object when they cruelly and unmercifully punish themselves in these emotional states which really call for kind and gentle treatment?

5. But we, my dear wife, have never needed to quarrel about the first of these types of extravagance and we shall not, I think, have to quarrel about the second either. Every philosopher who has ever been with us and shared our company has been amazed by the plain and modest way you dress and the simplicity of your general way of life, and at religious ceremonies, at sacrifices and at the theatre you have provided every citizen of our town with something else worth looking at – your own self-restraint. But then also you have already shown in times like this one your great powers of balance and control. I am thinking of when you lost your eldest child and then again when our lovely child Charon left us. I remember that on that occasion there were some people who had travelled back with me from the coast and that they came to our house with the rest when they heard of the child's death. What they found there was an atmosphere of peace and calm and, as they told others afterwards, they thought that some false rumours had got about and that nothing terrible had happened. And this was because you kept such wise and good order in the household at a time when just

the opposite could have happened; and yet you had nursed him at your own breast and had had to have an operation when your nipple was bruised. That was noble behaviour and it showed real love.

6. Most mothers, as we can see, behave differently. They let other people wash and tidy up their children and then take them into their arms as though they were pets; and when they die, they abandon themselves to empty and unbecoming grief that does not spring from real affection (for that is something reasonable and good), but from a combination of a little natural emotion with a great deal of empty fantasy which gives a wild and hysterical character to their grief and makes it difficult to check. Aesop seems to have noticed this. He said that when Zeus was distributing their honours to the gods, Grief also asked for a share. Zeus granted it, but said it should only come from those who voluntarily chose to give it. And at the beginning this is quite true; each person lets grief in of his own accord. But once it has had time to settle in and to become a constant and daily companion, it will not go away however much one wants to get rid of it. So we ought to resist it at the threshold and not let it come in and occupy the place; and this means not wearing mourning or cutting the hair off or doing any of the things which we see every day and which seem to frown at us and make our minds bitter and cramped, shut in on themselves, unapproachable and frightened of what is outside; the feeling, no doubt, is that once the clothes and the gestures of mourning have been adopted, one is debarred from laughter and daylight and the hospitality of friends. And this miserable state leads to neglect of the body; people will avoid baths and rubbing themselves down with oil and all the normal routine of life. But what ought to happen is just the opposite; a mind in distress needs the help of a healthy body. Just as the sea grows smooth in fair weather, much too of the misery of the mind will be

soothed and relaxed in the streams of calm that come from a body in good health. But if during these times the body becomes all parched and shrivelled from daily ill-usage and if instead of anything good or useful all it can impart to the soul is a kind of bitter and unwholesome exhalation of pain and sorrow, then the soul, as the result of such ill treatment will be in the grip of a kind of emotionalism from which, even if it wants to, it will find it hard to escape.

7. Yet I am not at all frightened of what is normally the worst and most formidable thing that can happen in these cases. I mean 'visits from women of the wrong sort'[4] with their wailing and their lamentations in chorus by which they rub the sore spot and exacerbate the pain and prevent it from dying down either of its own accord or from outside influences. I know well what a struggle you had yourself recently when you went to give your help to Theon's sister and had to fight off the invasion of the women from outside who with all their wailing and screaming were just 'putting fire on the fire'. It seems that when people see that their friends' houses are on fire they will rush up and do their best to put it out, but when it is a question of having one's heart on fire, they will just pile on more fuel. And when someone has an infection in the eye, people won't let anyone who wants to come and touch the sore place nor will they lay hands on it themselves; but the man who is mourning sits still and lets every passer-by finger and aggravate the soreness in his heart, rubbing it and scratching it until it breaks out into a wider and more serious infection. I know quite well that you will guard against anything of this sort.

8. But I should like you to try to carry yourself back in your thoughts into the past and often to recall the time when this little child had not yet been born and when we had as yet no reason to complain against fortune; then try to set this

4. Euripides, *Andromache*, 930.

present time alongside that one and imagine that things had again become just the same with us now as they were then. Will it not look, my dear wife, as though we were sorry that our child was even born, if we conclude that we were better off before her birth than we are now? We must not expunge from our memory those two years between her birth and her death; they gave us the joy and delight of her and should be counted among our pleasures; we should not consider the small good a great evil and we should not, if fortune did not add what we hoped for, be ungrateful for what was given us. Reverent language towards the divine power and a cheerful and uncomplaining attitude towards fortune will always bear sweet and noble fruit; and in times like these the man who draws most upon the memory of the good things and, turning his mind away from what is dark and disturbing, looks instead on the bright and shining part of his life will either get rid of his pain altogether, or, by blending it with its opposite, will lessen it and make it less intense. It is like perfume, which is always pleasant to smell and is often useful in counteracting bad smells; so to remember the good things in times of trouble gives us additional and necessary help, that is if we do not shrink from remembering our happiness and are not constantly blaming fortune for each and every thing. These are not the feelings we ought to have, complaining about the whole book of our life because one page has got a blot on it, while all the rest is clean and clear.

9. You have often heard that happiness depends on right reason resulting in a habit of stability and that no change of fortune can make any tremendous difference or undermine and ruin the basis of our lives.

But if we too must be like everyone else and be governed by external circumstances in our reckoning of fortune's dealings with us, and if we are to take the opinion of our neighbours as a criterion of happiness, then instead of letting your mind dwell on the way your visitors are indulging in a stupid and indiscriminate convention, what you ought to think of is how these same people still envy you for your children, your home and your whole way of life. Others would gladly choose to have your lot, even with our present sorrow; would it not be very unreasonable of you, who have this lot, to complain and be miserable about it? Better to learn from the very pain we now feel what great joys are still left to us and not be like those critics of Homer who pick out all the lines they call 'headless' or 'tail-less' and pay no attention to all the wonderfully and perfectly written passages. So, if you keep on singling out and complaining about the things that have gone wrong in your life, but will not give the same careful attention to the good things, you will be showing something rather like the illiberal spirit of a miser, who does nothing useful with all his wealth while he has it, but is wretched and heartbroken when he loses it.

And, if you feel pity for her because she has died without having been married and without having had children, then you can find some consolation in this thought, that you your-self have been both a wife and a mother. One must not think of these blessings as being so very important if one has been deprived of them and as not important if one has actually enjoyed them. She has entered into a state where there is no pain, and that is not something which ought to cause us pain. How can she cause suffering to us, if there is nothing now that can make her suffer? Even the loss of the most important things in life will cease to hurt us once we no longer feel the need for them. But your Timoxena's loss was a loss of little things; these were all she knew and it was in these that she found her pleasure. As for those things which she had never felt, which had never entered her head and of which she had no conception, she cannot really be said to have been deprived of these.

10. Then there are these others[5] who say that nothing evil or painful is at all possible in 'what has undergone dissolution'. Many people find them convincing, but I know that you will be prevented from believing in them by the doctrine of our fathers and by the experience which we share together of the revelations in the mysteries of Dionysus. We know that the soul is indestructable and should think that its experience is like that of a bird in a cage; if it has been kept in the body for a long time and become tamed to this life as a result of all sorts of involvements and long habituation it will alight again back to the body and for birth after birth will never stop or give up becoming entangled in the passions and chances of this world. It is not, and you must not think so, wrinkles, grey hair or bodily weakness that gives old age its bad name and reputation; the worst thing about it is this: that it sours and turns stale the soul's memories of the other world and makes it cling to this one, distorting it and cramping it through its eagerness to retain the shape that it has taken from the body. But the soul, that after being caged [in the body only stays so for a short time and is then set free][6] by higher powers, comes back again to its natural state, as though it had been only very slightly and very gently twisted out of shape. If you put a fire out and then light it again immediately, it will light up at once and soon be burning again; [but if you leave it out for a long time it will be much harder to rekindle. So with those souls which, as the poet says:][7]

Make haste to journey through the gates of Death[8]

before becoming deeply attached to earthly things and before becoming, as it were, melted down and chemically blended with the body.

5. The Epicureans.

6. These words represent the probable sense of a short lacuna in the text.

7. Probable sense of a lacuna in the text.   8. Theognis, 427.

11. The truth about all this is better shown in the customs and laws which have been handed down to us from the past. It is not our way to pour out libations for children who die in infancy, nor to perform the other ceremonies which the living do for the dead. This is because these infants are in no way involved with earth or earthly things; and so people do not stand around long at their funerals or keep watch at the tombs or at the laying out or at the side of the bodies. The laws do not allow us to . . .[9] for children of that age, indicating that in the case of those who have gone away to a better place and a more divine portion it is irreverent to . . .[10]

It is easier to believe this than to disbelieve it, and so let us act in our outward behaviour as the laws tell us and in our inner lives let us be still freer from stain, still purer and wiser than we were before.

9. Lacuna.   10. Lacuna.

Some other Penguin Classics are described
on the following pages.

FALL OF THE ROMAN REPUBLIC

Plutarch

TRANSLATED BY REX WARNER

Plutarch, as Rex Warner observes in introducing his modern translation of six of the *Lives,* was the last of the Greek classical historians and the first of modern biographers. Looking back from the turn of the first century A.D. he records, simply and dramatically, in the lives of Marius and Sulla, Crassus and Cicero, Pompey and Caesar, that long and bloody period of foreign and civil war which marked the collapse of the Roman Republic and ushered in the Empire. This volume forms a companion to the nine Greek lives of *The Rise and Fall of Athens* in the Penguin Classics.

MAKERS OF ROME

Plutarch

TRANSLATED BY IAN SCOTT-KILVERT

In his *Lives* Plutarch showed himself to be not only an inspired portrait-painter but a social historian of lasting importance. For *Makers of Rome* Ian Scott-Kilvert has selected nine of the Roman lives, from the earliest years of the Republic to the establishment of the Empire, to illustrate the courage and tenacity of the Romans in war and their genius for political compromise. These nine include the three Shakespearean heroes, Coriolanus, Brutus, and Mark Antony.

THE RISE AND FALL OF ATHENS

Plutarch

TRANSLATED BY IAN SCOTT-KILVERT

Writing at the turn of the first century A.D., Plutarch intentionally blended two cultures in his parallel lives of Greek and Roman heroes. The nine biographies chosen for this modern translation by Ian Scott-Kilvert illustrate the rise and fall of Athens from the legendary days of Theseus, the city's founder, to the age of Pericles and the razing of its walls by Lysander. The volume forms a companion to Plutarch's *Fall of the Roman Republic* in the Penguin Classics.

However unreliable in places, Plutarch's readable accounts have necessarily been a prime source of much historical knowledge.

THE PENGUIN CLASSICS

The Most Recent Volumes